Memories
of the
Old Plantation Home

by
Laura Locoul Gore

&

A Creole Family Album

Commentary by
Norman & Sand Marmillion

The Zoë Company, Inc.
Vacherie, Louisiana
2007

Library of Congress Cataloging-in-Publication Data
Gore, Laura Locoul, 1861-1963
Memories of the old plantation home/ by Laura Locoul Gore.
A Creole family album / commentary by Norman & Sand Marmillion. --3rd ed.
p. cm.
ISBN 0-9705591-0-0
1. Gore, Laura Locoul, 1861-1963.
2. Locoul family.
3. Plantation life--Louisiana--St. James Parish--History--19th Century
4. Creoles--Louisiana--History
5. St. James Parish, (La.)--Social life and customs.
I. Marmillion, Norman J. II. Marmillion, Sand.
III. Title.   IV. Title: Creole family album.

F377.S134G67 2000   976.3'31'0922
                          QBI00-901622

10 9 8

Printed in Louisiana,
United States of America

Cover: Manor house, Duparc & Locoul Plantation in the 1870s, Vacherie, Louisiana

The Zoë Company, Inc.
P.O. Box 38
Vacherie LA 70090
email: thezoeco@aol.com

PREFACE

In July, 1993, the editors of this work first saw and read the only manuscript of <u>Memories of the Old Plantation Home</u>, written by Laura Locoul Gore. With this unexpected discovery, a window into Louisiana's Creole past was opened. Before her death in St. Louis, Missouri in 1963, Mrs. Gore handed her writings over to her two daughters. And, when the Gore daughters themselves became aged and feeble, they, likewise, gave the manuscripts to a trusted friend, telling him to safeguard their family stories and that, some day, someone would surely contact him from Louisiana in search of their mother's writings. For 14 more years Mrs. Gore's writings were kept by the Gore's friend, until the editors of this book happened upon them in search of photographs of an old, abandoned sugar plantation in Louisiana called "Laura."

The manuscript, which Laura Locoul Gore completed in 1936, recounts the daily life and major events in the lives of her parents, grandparents and great-grandparents, as well as that of workers, slaves and children, all of whom resided or influenced life on the sugar plantation that today bears the name: Laura Plantation. Laura's <u>Memories</u> give readers an in-depth, insider's look into a Creole household. Hers is a story of French aristocrats, Creole colonials, war heroes, astute business women, stoic slaves and bored childhoods. Her <u>Memories</u> span four generations of love and greed, of heroism and pettiness, of pride and betrayal, violence and excess, each generation dealing differently with a disintegrating culture. Moreover, it is a story written by Laura to explain to her children why she would, even at an early age, reject the traditional, immoderate and extended familial confines of the Creole world. Laura's personal choice was in favor of what she saw as her own individual future: life as a modern, liberated American woman, in the new and changing 20th Century.

The life that Laura gave up to marry a Protestant from St. Louis, Missouri, was one that is quite alien to the early 21st Century American. The Creole way of life, long established before Louisiana became a part of the United States in 1803 and, for two hundred years the dominant lifestyle in south Louisiana, has all but vanished. Creole Louisiana was not so much a biological phenomenon as it was a cultural milieu. Laura's family, wholly of French and French-Canadian blood, shared a history and value system more closely aligned with that of the slaves and tenant farmers on her family plantation than that of the neighboring Anglo plantation owners of the same upper economic class.

Born out of the desperation of French colonial policy and influenced greatly by other European, French-Canadian, West-African and native Indian inhabitants, a Creole World was born in Louisiana by the early 18th Century. Strikingly similar to other Creole cultures across the globe, Louisiana's was a thorough blending of disparate cultures, creating a lifestyle that was new and different. It was greatly influenced and affiliated with its parent cultures, all the while having little of the contributing cultures predominate.

Though French in language and administration, and later Spanish in official manifestation, this hybrid culture initiated a novel way of thinking and living. From the first decades of European settlement, Louisiana's children quickly adapted, economically, socially and politically, to the harsh realities of survival in the isolated backwater of Louisiana. It was these mutations which became the visible icons of the Louisiana Creole well into the 20th Century. The children of these various ethnic groups and nationalities, that is, to say, the first Creole generation in Louisiana, shared a common value system, quite distinct from that of the white-Anglo-Saxon-Protestant ethic which would, from 1803 onward, aggressively impose itself upon and subvert the local Creole.

While the Creole was, with justification, labeled elitist and undemocratic by American neighbors, no descriptive image suited the Creoles better than that they were, first and foremost, family-centered. Early Louisiana history taught her first immigrants the irrelevancy of the European necessities of religion, race, gender and national origin and, in their places, posited the family as the principal determinant of survival and fulfillment.

By the 1780s, the plantation economy was beginning to overpower subsistence farming and the Creole family network was already playing the kingmaker role in the economy, society and politics of Louisiana. From early on, the Creole families were linked in business relationships throughout the state and their business was conducted, for the most part, within the family. Everyone in the family, young included, was considered a member of the family enterprise and the plantation became the corporate headquarters for the family business.

By the time Laura's great-grandmother became the president of the family plantation enterprise in 1808, there had long existed the Creole tradition of women as plantation owners and managers. Laura's grandmother followed the tradition as well, running the plantation for almost 47 years. When Laura's father named the plantation for her, Laura was only 13 years old. She found herself confronted with the reality that she, one day, would be thrust into the same, demanding Creole roles as her female predecessors.

The images Laura gives us of her family range wildly from the sensitive to the brutal, traits that reappear in each succeeding generation, a truly frightening prospect for a teenage girl who was expected to accept responsibility for it all. Laura's decision to escape the heavy burdens of family history seems, to the American mind, a natural, suitable and inevitable one for her. For modern readers, her decision will be seen as a classic model of psychological maturity.

By her own account, Laura succeeded in living a fulfilled adult life outside the familiarity of the Creole world, just as she dreamed she could. Yet, throughout her many years, she found herself being drawn back to the old plantation, almost to the point of obsession. Having left the plantation at age 29, Laura never left her fascination with and affection for the farm, the ancient, rigid life style, New Orleans, her countless French-speaking relatives and her childhood friends. Laura would make one, final return to the Laura Plantation for a farewell visit in the summer of 1931. In 1936, after five years of writing, at age 74, she completed her <u>Memories of the Old Plantation Home</u>.

As was the custom in Creole Louisiana, Laura, like all eldest daughters, was entrusted with collecting and safeguarding the family history, photographs, heirlooms, etc. in order to pass them down to the next generation. Laura kept true to this tradition and compiled her memoirs for her children who had only a skeletal knowledge of the family and its genealogy. As a young girl, she listened to stories told to her by her mother and paternal grandmother, both of whom played major, detailed roles in her pages. Throughout her long life, Laura kept biographical notes on family members as well as vignettes on daily life in New Orleans and on the plantation. But, her <u>Memories</u> are neither a diary nor a journal, as she only started to write recollections of her life in Louisiana when she was elderly, living in St. Louis in the 1930s.

For more than six decades, Laura Gore filled four large family photograph albums, squeezing them full of marginal notations, scholastic report cards, love letters, legal papers, holy picture cards, newspaper articles, and fragments of communion and wedding dresses. Excerpts of these writings have been included in the <u>Memories</u> as well as many of the images she collected.

It seems that it was almost exclusively from oral histories and from her own experiences that Laura derived her <u>Memories of the Old Plantation Home</u>, and not from any outside written sources. Most probably, she did not know many of the facts which have later been uncovered about her family and their farm. Therefore, the second part of this book, <u>A Creole Family Album</u>, attempts to complement Laura's writings with materials gathered from sources not readily accessible to her, presenting a broader biographical and photographic description of her family and the Creole world.

Upon reading Laura's manuscripts and drafts, one finds that she re-edited her <u>Memories</u> over a long period of time. In some cases, she only hinted at unpleasantries and the sins of her family. In other cases, she evidently did not want her readers (her children) to clearly know what had happened.   In 1947, she wrote again, this time a much abridged (only 10 pages), highly-censored, version of her <u>Memories</u>, done at the request of her French cousins. This second writing included no new information but did leave out whole chapters and any reference that could possibly discomfort her French cousins as it related to the lives of their parents and grandparents. Laura's <u>Memories</u> abruptly concludes in 1891 with her decision to marry and leave her Creole plantation and Louisiana. So, <u>A Creole Family Album</u> also examines, in the briefest manner, the 72 years of Laura's life following her wedding, about which, as far as we know, she left no written testimony.

Despite the limitations listed above, Laura's words still manage to convey an intimate look into the lives of real individuals, all from the same family, over a 200-year span, all living in a world apart from the American mainstream. We in the 21st Century, especially we who live in Louisiana and in the United States, owe Laura Locoul Gore a belated debt of gratitude because, what she knew, she wrote down for her children and for us, too.

Norman & Sand Marmillion

ACKNOWLEDGEMENTS ❧ *REMERCIEMENTS*

In August of 1993, we acquired 13+ acres of a long-abandoned plantation homestead on the River Road between New Orleans and Baton Rouge. Our goal was to restore its standing structures and to open it as a tourist attraction. In attempting to find whatever information existed about the site, we interviewed members of the Waguespack family. The Waguespacks had lived on-site for 90 years and were graciously forthcoming in what they knew of the farm they called "Laura" or "Waguespack plantation." But, in all our interviews, we could not find one photograph of the place that predated the 1940s, the Waguespack photographs having been lost in a fire.

Miss Elmire "Mimi" Waguespack, one of the last sisters to live on-site, invited us to her home. As we looked through her scrapbooks for an old view of the big house, she pointed out a letter dated 1967; a letter she believed was sent by someone in the first family to own "Laura." The short letter said, "We had a wonderful visit. My mother-in-law always told us it was a fine place. Here are our addresses. Thank you for your hospitality." Below were listed three addresses: one in St. Louis, Missouri, one in Morristown, New Jersey and one from Paris, France. We wrote down the addresses.

We sent letters to the three, asking if they had photos of "Laura." The St. Louis letter, addressed to a Mrs. Charles Gore, was returned, unopened, "address unknown." Morristown's reply was that "my parents have died but visited 'Laura' in 1967 along with its original owners." When the Paris letter arrived, it read, "Sorry, I do not know about what you write. My mother, to whom you wrote, just died last month, aged 98."

On a trip to the New Orleans public library we copied all the "Gores" in the St. Louis telephone directory. Once home, we started to call everyone (64 names). Each call began the same, "Hello, we're looking for photographs of a place in Louisiana called Laura Plantation. Can you help us?" On the 62nd call, we reached Stephen Gore, grandson of Laura Locoul Gore. Stephen had no photographs but offered us vital leads and information for our quest. One such lead was Myra Ancira in New Orleans.

We asked Myra the familiar "photo question." She had no images but, since Myra's family and Laura's had been close for generations, she offered to send us a copy of her grandmother's address book, filled with names of mutual friends in New Orleans and St. Louis. We started with "A" and headed for "Z." Most were the names of deceased friends. Under "N" we called Clyde Norris, in St. Louis. Upon asking the same "photo question," Clyde paused and then said, "I have been waiting fourteen years for a phone call from Louisiana. Are you the caller I have been waiting for?" To which I replied, "I am." Without hesitation, Clyde said, "Then you must come up to St. Louis to see what I've been holding for you all these years."

5

At his home, Clyde had covered his dining table with an array of scrapbooks, photographs, silver and old boxes and, at the far end of the table, he had positioned a black-bound manuscript entitled <u>Memories of the Old Plantation Home</u> by Laura Locoul Gore. "All this is yours," he said. "I was told to keep it until you came or, in the event of my death, I was to will it to the Missouri Historical Society." On the road to New Orleans, we read and re-read the memoirs. We wrote back to the Paris address, to Sophie Maugras, now knowing that she was Laura's cousin. Sophie quickly responded by offering us access to two weighty dossiers of information relating to her family and the sugar plantation, all safeguarded in the *Archives Nationales* in Paris. Many letters from Sophie followed, each containing wonderful old portraits, momentos and, *voilà*, photographs of the old plantation.

These people, Mimi Waguespack, Stephen Gore, Myra Ancira, Sophie Maugras and, foremost, Clyde Norris deserve the greatest acknowledgement for the existence of this publication. All were kind and generous to us, who were strangers to them at the time. Both Mimi Waguespack and Clyde Norris have recently died. It is to their memory that we dedicate this book.

It would be impossible to thank everyone who helped us in this publication. Among those to whom we are particularly indebted are first, Louise Coleman. Louise worked with us, for months on end, in the earliest stages of research and drafting of the commentary. Many a night we ate at her table and computer, thrashing out <u>A Creole Family Album</u>. Our research relied heavily upon the efforts of Alfred Lemmon of The Historic New Orleans Collection and our work in St. Louis was successful due to the on-going research and hospitality of Emory and Jane Webre. Advice and research also came from Wilbert Waguespack, Jr., Linda Thomas, Bobbie DeBlieux, Gregory Osborne, Mrs. Lucille Prud'Homme, Clifford Burns, Lee Warren, Anthony Tassin, Madeline Axtman, Noah Robert, Shannon Dawdy, Elizabeth Shoup, Maurice Meslans, Elizabeth McMillan, Betty Hertzog, Messiane de Crouy-Chanel, Marguerite de Bellescize Paget and the Friends of *Vieilles Maisons Françaises*, Glynne Couvillion, Paul Nevski, Eugene Cizek and Warren Norris.

Photograph and illustration credits go out to Leonce Haydel and the St. James Historical Society, Neal Auction Company of New Orleans, Mary Breazeale Cunningham of Shreveport, Gene Beyt of Baton Rouge, Peter Patout of New Orleans, Syndey Byrd of New Orleans, Arthur Hardy of New Orleans, The Greenbrier of White Sulphur Springs, West Virginia, Hilda Haydel Waguespack of Vacherie, Gabriel Thépaut of Ste. Honorine du Fay, Normandie and William Coble of New Orleans. Technical, computer, printing and translation consultations were generously offered by Barbara Allen, Stephen DuPlantier, Marie Rudd, Ernest Posey, Sonia Cohen and Isabelle de Vendeuvre.

A debt of gratitude goes to our families, to members of the Laura Plantation Company and, of course, to the staff at Laura Plantation whose constant urging and advice were always appreciated and who continue to give the "best history tour in the U.S." Lastly, a warm hug, kiss and thanks goes to Françoise Zoë "Frannie," our dearest daughter, who, for countless days and nights, has seen our attention diverted to this publication. We thank you all.

DUPARC-LOCOUL
FAMILY CHART

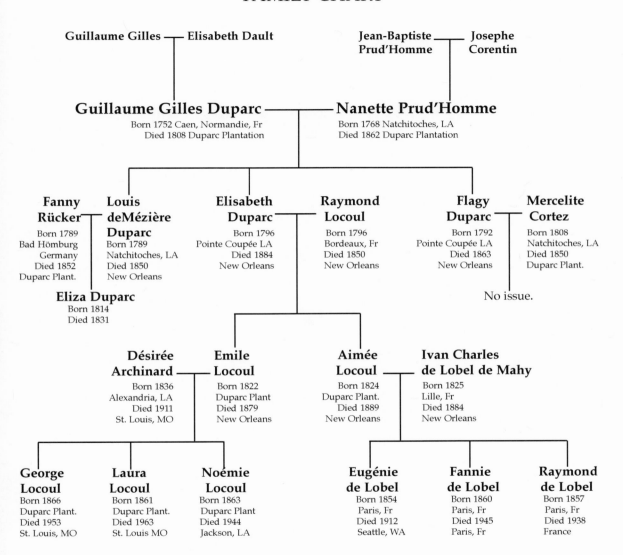

Guillaume Gilles —— Elisabeth Dault

Jean-Baptiste —— Josephe
Prud'Homme   Corentin

Guillaume Gilles Duparc —— **Nanette Prud'Homme**

Born 1752 Caen, Normandie, Fr
Died 1808 Duparc Plantation

Born 1768 Natchitoches, LA
Died 1862 Duparc Plantation

**Fanny
Rücker**

Born 1789
Bad Hömburg
Germany
Died 1852
Duparc Plant.

**Louis
deMézière
Duparc**

Born 1789
Natchitoches, LA
Died 1850
New Orleans

**Elisabeth
Duparc**

Born 1796
Pointe Coupée LA
Died 1884
New Orleans

**Raymond
Locoul**

Born 1796
Bordeaux, Fr
Died 1850
New Orleans

**Flagy
Duparc**

Born 1792
Pointe Coupée LA
Died 1863
New Orleans

**Mercelite
Cortez**

Born 1808
Natchitoches, LA
Died 1850
Duparc Plant.

Eliza Duparc

Born 1814
Died 1831

No issue.

**Désirée
Archinard**

Born 1836
Alexandria, LA
Died 1911
St. Louis, MO

**Emile
Locoul**

Born 1822
Duparc Plant
Died 1879
New Orleans

**Aimée
Locoul**

Born 1824
Duparc Plant.
Died 1889
New Orleans

**Ivan Charles
de Lobel de Mahy**

Born 1825
Lille, Fr
Died 1884
New Orleans

**George
Locoul**

Born 1866
Duparc Plant.
Died 1953
St. Louis, MO

**Laura
Locoul**

Born 1861
Duparc Plant.
Died 1963
St. Louis MO

**Noémie
Locoul**

Born 1863
Duparc Plant
Died 1944
Jackson, LA

**Eugénie
de Lobel**

Born 1854
Paris, Fr
Died 1912
Seattle, WA

**Fannie
de Lobel**

Born 1860
Paris, Fr
Died 1945
Paris, Fr

**Raymond
de Lobel**

Born 1857
Paris, Fr
Died 1938
France

7

First page of Laura Gore's manuscript, 1936

Memories of the old Plantation
home in St James Parish Louisiana
on the right bank of the Mississippi river
——————— abt 54 miles above New Orleans.

St Louis Mo. January 1936
at 5921 de Giverville ave.

Dedicated to my three Children Laura Ann Gore,
Désirée Loeral Gore, & Charles H. Gore Jr—

At the Earnest insistance of my three Children
Lollie, Daisie, & Charlie Jr. that I write the
memories of my childhood days on the old plantation
in Louisiana In them. I have continued to
do so — before my memory begins to fail me, — for
I realize that I am the last one of my generation
in the family left. who truly and where of the
of the life in the South as I knew it, & any of the
old plantation home where I first saw the light
of day — and where my father — and his mother and
others also. I made my arrival, as a Christmas
gift — (so it would seem) to my parents, on the 24th
of December (Tuesday) at six oclock in the
morning — and narrowly escaped being called Noelie
of account of Noel, Christmas.
Before I proceed with my own recollections — it
is only fitting that I should mention the facts about
my ancestors — as I remember them from my Grandmother

*Memories of the old plantation
home in St. James Parish, Louisiana
on the right bank of the Mississippi River*

---

and 54 miles above New Orleans

---

*St. Louis, Mo.   January 1936
at 5921 de Giverville Ave.*

---

*Dedicated to my three Children: Laura Ann Gore,
Désirée Locoul Gore & Charles H. Gore, Jr.*

At *the earnest insistence of my three children, Lollie, Daisie and Charlie, Jr., I write the memories of my childhood days on the old plantation in Louisiana for them.*

I have concluded to do so, before my memory begins to fail me, for I realize that I am the last one of my generation left who could tell them of life in the South as I knew it, and of the old plantation home where I first saw the light of day, and where my father and his mother were born, also.

I made my arrival as a Christmas gift (so it would seem) to my parents on the 24th of December (Tuesday) at six o'clock in the morning and narrowly escaped being called "Noëlie" of account of Noël (Christmas).

Before I proceed with my own recollections, it is only fitting that I should mention some facts about my ancestors as I remember them from (or as was told to me by) my grandmother. I have no written proofs of these facts, nor exact notes, for Grandmother often said that the old Court House at Pointe Coupée had burned down, with all valuable papers destroyed. But her statements are sure to be accurate for she was a young woman when her father died and knew the whole of what she spoke.

Laura Locoul Gore

GUILLAUME DuPARC

My grandmother's father, my great-grandfather, Le Général Guillaume Duparc, had come over when Rochambeau and LaFayette offered their services to this Country.

Guillaume Gilles Duparc

My cousin, Aimée d'Abzac Maugras, wrote me the following story of how our ancestor came to America: "It was after a duel. Duparc was born in Caen and his father must have had land somewhere near. Duparc killed a young man who was his father's best friend's son. In anger, his father fired his gun at him but missed him and killed his favorite cow. That was in Normandy where there are many cows."

From what my mother and my Aunt Aimée de Lobel told me, I understand that Duparc joined Admiral de Grasse's Navy or was sent over by order of his father. At that time, at the end of the 18th Century, dueling was not very popular in France, especially duels which resulted in the death of a man.

Duparc fought under the Spanish Admiral Bernardo de Galvez against the British in 1778 at the Battle of Pensacola, Florida where he distinguished himself and was later acknowledged by the Spanish King Carlos. Guillaume Duparc was wounded at Yorktown. From 1792 until 1803, Duparc was Spanish colonial *Commandante* of the Pointe Coupée Post in central Louisiana. He was given grants of land for his services and later, in about 1804, drifted to St. James Parish on the right bank of the Mississippi River, 54 miles above New Orleans, where the Duparc & Locoul plantation is situated and where three generations of my family were born.

NANETTE PRUD'HOMME

Le *Général* Guillaume Duparc married Anne "Nanette" Prud'Homme, from the northern part of Louisiana. She was related to the large and ancient Prud'Homme family there. The Prud'Hommes in this country all come from Dr. Jean Prud'Homme, *"médecin de sa Majeste Louis XV,"* who had been the court physician of Louis XV, and later came to this country and settled in Louisiana. Nanette Prud'Homme's father, Jean-Baptiste, was a physician by profession and, for some time, held the position of "king's doctor" at the old French military post of Fort St. Jean-Baptiste, where the city of Natchitoches now stands. Nanette's brother, Emmanuel Prud'Homme also lived in Natchitoches where many of his descendants still live.

Chapel,
Fort St. Jean-Baptiste,
Natchitoches, LA
(reconstructed)

My great-grandmother, Nanette Prud'Homme, died at the age of 94. When she died, I was a very tiny infant and she was in her "second childhood." Of this dear, old lady, I must tell some of the amusing things said and done by her in her later years. Nanette called her daughter (my grandmother), "Maman" and would cry and fight as a child with her nurse, not to be put to bed at night, until my grandmother intervened.

When questioned about her youth, she would answer coyly, *"Non, je n'etais pas jolie, mais j'avais un teint de roses."* "No, I was not pretty, but I did have a complexion of roses." Then, upon further questioning, she would say, "I have small hands and feet." And, "Oh, how terrible it was at a dance one night when a tall, gauchy American asked me to dance and mashed my toe." And looking at her toe, she would say, "To this day my toe still hurts me." The reference to the "gauchy American" was not meant to be in any way complimentary, for none but a gallant Frenchman was to be considered a gentleman.

As was her custom in the morning, she would take her rosary and walk up and down the long gallery saying her beads and singing the French national anthem: *"Allons enfants de la patrie, le jour de gloire est arrivé."*

Nanette called my mother *"la grande dame en noir"* because, for years, my mother was in mourning dress for her own mother. And, when I was introduced to my great-grandmother, she refused to believe I was my father's infant, as she considered him still the little child she had loved so dearly. Nanette had three children: Louis "de Mézière" Duparc, Guillaume Flagy Duparc and Elisabeth Duparc, who is my grandmother.

Nanette Prud'Homme Duparc
age 82
photograph taken at the Duparc Plantation 1850

LOUIS de MÉZIERE DuPARC

I never knew where the name "de Mézière" came from but was interested in a queer coincidence. While reading Lyle Saxon's <u>History of Louisiana</u>, I saw that a "Marquis de Mézière" had come over during the Colonial Wars and was stationed at Pointe Coupée in central Louisiana where my great-grandfather was commandante at the same time. Whether an intimacy started between them and Duparc named his eldest son for the Marquis, or they had been friends in Europe, I do not know, but, certainly, the coincidence attracted me.

Louis de Mézière Duparc

Louis de Mézière Duparc was sent to France to be educated. As a young man, he was known in Louisiana as the "Fire-eater," for his violent temper. He attended the military college in Bordeaux and remained there for many years. His mother refused to send him any more funds until he returned to this country.

When he came back, he was married to Fannie Rücker, of Bad Hömburg, Germany, a charming, elegant, beautiful and Paris-educated girl who captured the whole family by her wonderful personality.

Fannie Rücker

Louis and Fannie had only one child, a daughter, Eliza. When Eliza was 16 years old they took her on a visit to Paris where they consulted a medical specialist. They wanted her to be perfect and, at times, she developed *"les boutons"* or pimples on her face. From the medical treatment, Eliza contracted a fever and died in a short while.

There is a little family gossip which you may believe or not, as you please. It seems that Louis' brother-in-law, who was my grandfather, Raymond Locoul, was in Paris at the same time and he had referred Louis to the specialist. Grandfather Raymond Locoul was sitting in an adjoining room where the doctors were holding a consultation about Eliza's treatment when he heard, *"Oui, mon ami, vous avez raison, j'ai fait une boulette!"* or, "Yes, my friend, you are right. I have made a mistake!"

Grandfather Raymond kept quiet about this until he returned home and told my grandmother Elisabeth. Never a word was breathed to the disconsolate parents because Louis, with his fiery disposition, would have the taken the doctor's life or injured him.

Before bringing their daughter's body back to this country, Louis and Fannie remained in Paris for a year so as to have her portrait painted from a plaster cast death mask of her face. Eliza's remains were brought back to America and are buried in the family tomb in St. James Parish.

Eliza Duparc
posthumous
portrait painted
in 1831 by
Cigelon

We have Eliza's portrait hanging in our parlor here in St. Louis, but it is much faded. The date of her death I saw on the family tomb was 1831. After the burial, Eliza's mother, Tante Fannie, never left her room in the big house of the plantation, even to go to her meals, but lived the life of a recluse until her death.

FLAGY DuPARC

Guillaume Flagy Duparc, the second son, never had the advantages of his elder brother, Louis, and refused to go to college. He begged to be allowed to manage the family plantation. His father had died and his mother, Nanette, yielded to his demand. He took charge and made the family fortune on the plantation. Flagy always felt this inferiority difference in his brother's education for he was shy, grouchy and uncongenial. His morose disposition led to many family difficulties and feuds.

He did marry a lovely girl, Mercelite Cortes, whom he adored. They had no children and Mercelite died many years before him. Before his wife's early death, they had adopted her niece, Odile Carr, who lived on the plantation with them and remained even after Mercelite's death. Flagy left Odile quite a bit of his fortune. She married a Dr. Kueneman who dissipated most of her inheritance in ventures in other plantations. Then, Kueneman and Odile returned to Europe where he became the Doctor to the Prince of Monaco. They had two children, a son and daughter, and I never heard of them since.

Maison de Reprise
at the
Laura Plantation
formerly known as the
Duparc & Locoul
Plantation

ELISABETH DuPARC

In 1822, my grandmother, Elisabeth Duparc, married George Raymond Locoul, a young Frenchman, whom she met in New Orleans while visiting her friends, the Labatut family. This young man had come to the States in 1821 with letters of introduction (and all his credentials) to Mr. Labatut before he was invited into the home of one of New Orleans' most prominent citizens. My grandmother was an heiress in her own name, and my grandfather, a polished gentleman of France. He courted and won her and they lived on the plantation.

Of the Locoul family, I know but little except that my Grandfather Locoul was an only son and that his father was an only child and that they lived in Bordeaux. My grandfather was beloved by all and an angel of peace dropped among a family of fire-eaters.

My grandfather had a most pleasing personality and charming manners. When tempers flew high among his spirited brothers-in-law, he always managed to be the pacifist of the family, and the two brothers loved him.

Elisabeth Duparc
wedding portrait
1822

At the death of her two brothers, my grandmother fully inherited the plantation and lived there with her husband and two children: Louis Raymond Emile Locoul, my father, and Aimée Locoul, his sister, who later married a Frenchman, Ivan de Lobel-Mahy.

Raymond Locoul
wedding portrait
1822

19

MY DEAR, OLD DAD

M y father, Louis Raymond "Emile" Locoul, was born at the old plantation home on December 20, 1822. At an early age, 13 years old, he was sent to Europe to begin his education *"au College Royale de Bordeaux,"* which was the *Lycée Militaire de Bordeaux*, a military college. He remained there until his graduation when his parents and his sister, Aimée, joined him in France. The family remained in Paris, while my father was given the present of a trip through Europe as reward for his graduation, and they then returned to America together.

It was related to me that when Father returned home to Louisiana and first met Désirée, his future wife, at a party, he told his sister, Aimée, "She is the one I am going to marry, if she will have me." To Father's words, Aimée replied, "You make up your mind very quickly."

Father wished to study law, of which he was very fond. I have no doubt he would have made his mark in the world as he had a brilliant mind and read extensively. Often Father would discuss the law with his plantation neighbor, Judge (later, Governor) Roman, and he could have passed the Bar examinations, if he so desired.

Emile Locoul
as a cadet
at the
Lycée Militaire,
Bordeaux,
age 14

But, the family opposed his going into law bitterly, for a "southern gentleman had to be a planter." Professional men were not regarded with favor, nor had the same prestige. When a sugar planter walked the streets of New Orleans with his cottonade britches, alpaca coat, panama hat and gold-headed cane, he was looked upon as the king of creation and everybody bowed down to him. My father spent most of his time between the plantation and New Orleans, leading the life of the average young gentleman of leisure of those days and making frequent trips to Europe to renew old friendships and acquaintances.

MY MOTHER'S FAMILY

My mother, Louise Désirée Archinard, was born on the old Metoyer Plantation (present-day Bermuda, Louisiana) in Natchitoches Parish, on September 20th, 1836. Her father was François Archinard, the son of John Archinard of Geneva, Switzerland, and of Louise Rappicault of St. Louis. The Archinards came from Geneva and settled on "Cotton Plantation" in Rapides Parish near Alexandria, Louisiana.

Of the children of John and Louise Archinard, grandfather François was the oldest of four brothers and two sisters. Of his brothers, Evariste married in Alexandria and had a large family. Jean-César married, but had no family, and the older brother, Richmond, remained a bachelor. François had two sisters: Désirée, who died in childhood, and Irène, who married Judge Henry Boyce (their two children: Louise and Henry Boyce.) Louise later married Powhatan Clark of Virginia and lived in Baltimore, Maryland.

My grandfather, François Archinard, was sent to Geneva, to an old uncle, John Archinard, to be educated in the land of his forefathers. He returned to America after reaching manhood, and became a cotton planter with one of his brothers in Rapides Parish near Alexandria, Louisiana.

François married my grandmother, Céphalide Metoyer, of Natchitoches, who was the daughter of F. Benjamin Metoyer and of Aurore Lambre, prominent cotton planters of that Parish. Céphalide was the eldest of 15 children. At an early age, she was sent to New Orleans to be educated at the Ursuline Convent, where she remained ten years without seeing her mother. At that time, transportation was long, difficult and slow.

François Archinard

Benjamin Metoyer, Céphalide's father, each year had his cotton crop boarded on a barge and, with friends and a chef, would drift down the river, stopping at many of the plantations on the way, reaching New Orleans at the end of a month. There he saw his daughter, sold his crop and stayed for Carnival, enjoying life to the fullest.

Benjamin was very friendly with the Locoul family and he dined with them frequently, while his wife remained with the brood of children at home on the cotton plantation. His jokes, pranks and general hilarity as a *"bon viveur"* were so well known that my grandmother, Elisabeth Locoul, always called him: *"le Diable de Benjamin."*

His daughter, Céphalide, frequently visited her Locoul cousins in the City (New Orleans) during her vacation, or spent the summer on our plantation. She adored the Locoul family. My father was then a very young child (in the mid-1820s). When Céphalide returned to the Metoyer Plantation near Natchitoches, she did not recognize her mother, having been away from home for so long a time.

Benjamin Metoyer, died a ruined man, having given security for a friend who failed to meet his obligations. Her poor, old, dear widowed mother, Aurore Lambre Metoyer; or "Mémée" (as her grandchildren and great-grandchildren called her), was left with this debt of $90,000, a family of 14 children to raise, and most of them only half-grown. The grand old lady buckled down to the strictest economy. Friends went to Washington, D.C. to have her freed from the interest, and she lived long enough to receive her cancelled note and have her cotton plantation free of mortgage.

Aurore Lambre
1789-1877

I must not fail to mention an original saying of my Grandmother Locoul, who was clever, witty and always quick at *répartie*. It happened at that time that many a warm-hearted planter had been a victim of signatures given as security to help out friends in distress. Some planters had lost their homes or fortunes or, in some cases, their lives from illness or worry. Grandmother, upon hearing of one case, exclaimed, making the Sign of the Cross, *"Je ne donne, ni ne prête, ni n'endosse pour personne,"* meaning, "I neither give nor lend nor endorse for anyone." This saying was a howling success and a slogan of hers for a long time.

Céphalide's husband, my grandfather, François Archinard, died when my mother, Désirée, was only 8 years old. He was one of the first victims of a cholera epidemic and was taken to New Orleans for treatment where he died in 1845. His body was taken to Rapides Parish for burial where he lies 10 feet underground in the family plot on the old Archinard Plantation near Alexandria.

After her husband's untimely death, my Grandmother Céphalide would have preferred being in Alexandria with her two daughters, Désirée, who is my mother, and her sister, my Aunt Irène. It was, at that time, contrary to custom and good form for a young widow to live alone with her children so, she had to return to Natchitoches to live with her mother (Mémée Aurore Lambre Metoyer) and the enormous family of sisters and brothers and their families.

Céphalide Metoyer

Désirée Archinard

My mother, Désirée, was sent to the Sacred Heart Convent in Natchitoches where she remained until her graduation. She was as great a favorite there as she was to become later, with all who knew her. Mother was pretty and bright, with the most lovable disposition. She sang and played delightfully and had perfect command of both English and French. Mother was the acknowledged belle of *"la Côte Joyeuse,"* as the settlement of Bermuda in Natchitoches Parish was called then, owing to the great number of fun-loving people, all related, who made the place so gay.

Ten years later, Grandmother Céphalide married her brother-in-law, Phanor Prud'Homme, whose children Céphalide had looked after and cared for after her sister's (Lise Metoyer's) death. This marriage made my mother very happy, as her Uncle Phanor, who was now her step-father, had loved her and had been a second father to her in her early youth. Grandmother Céphalide and mother lived on Oakland, the Prud'Homme Plantation, not far from Bermuda.

The oldest daughter of Phanor, Adeline, was my mother's bosom friend and, in 1854, when they were both 18 years of age, "Grandfather" Phanor took them both to New York and through the Eastern U.S. on a summer vacation. It was a habit in those days then, when one family planned to go anywhere, others immediately decided to accompany them. So, quite a merry party of young people went on the same trip. I believe that Mother wanted Father to come along with them on this trip, chaperoned.

During this trip, the Prud'Homme party remained a few days in New Orleans. Grandmother, Elisabeth Duparc Locoul, who was Phanor's cousin, entertained them at dinner at her house on Toulouse Street. My father, 32 years old, was returning from the plantation and his boat was late in landing, so much so that when he arrived at the house, the dinner was nearly over.

*Phanor Prud'Homme
and his son,
Emmanuel*

Upon entering the dining room, Father made his salutations and spoke to the elder ladies first. Then, hastily crossing to Mother's side, he said to her, "I need no introduction to you. I know you are the daughter of my dear friend, Céphalide." Mother was much confused and embarrassed at being singled out, because she knew there would be no end of teasing and comment from those of her party who had witnessed the meeting.

For the rest of their stay in New Orleans, my father, who was most arduous in his attentions, was Devotion itself, sending flowers, escorting her to the Opera, etc. Before she left for the Northeast, he confided in her his feelings, but she was not to be had for the asking and refused to give him an answer until she should return to her home. And there, he should come and woo her.

A great little episode was told that, as my mother stepped off the boat that brought them back to New Orleans from their trip to the Northeast, a young man, standing on the levee to see the boat land, spied the group and, walking up to my step-grandfather, Phanor Prud'Homme, said, "Pardon me, sir, but by the resemblance, I believe this young lady to be a relative of mine. My name is Alfred Archinard and I am the son of Evariste Archinard of Alexandria. Phanor then extended his hand and told him the young lady was indeed his first cousin.

Alfred joined the party and was with them constantly, showering as much attention on Mother as he was permitted to by my father, much to the annoyance of both men, who eyed each other very suspiciously. Strange, but that history was to repeat itself many years later with Alfred's son and Mother's daughter (Me!), with the same result that the other man won out!

Oakland Plantation, Natchitoches Parish

One month later, my father, Emile Locoul, wrote asking permission to visit Phanor Prud'Homme's home at Oakland Plantation. The invitation was extended, with the result that an engagement soon followed. Father made several visits to Natchitoches, which was a very tedious trip in those days, taking three days by boat to get there.

The marriage, though, had to be postponed for Grandmother Céphalide was taken quite ill. She had suffered a stroke and was paralyzed. Céphalide had married Phanor at a critical age and had given birth to a little daughter, Mignonne, who lived only six months, and this was supposed to be the cause of her illness. My mother, Désirée, nursed her own mother with all the tenderness and love that she was capable of and, in consequence, was very much fatigued.

It was decided, when Father was visiting there, that the wedding should take place at once and that they should go immediately to New Orleans and secure suitable accommodations in a boarding house, for Grandfather Phanor had planned to take his wife Céphalide there for treatment under the then famous Dr. Home.

Désirée Locoul's engagement photo

The *"Corbeille de Noce,"* the bridal outfit, was always given by the groom and had arrived several months before, with gifts of jewels from each member of the Locoul family. Mother was married at her Grandmother Metoyer's plantation home in Bermuda, with only the family attending. She wore a lovely *Mousseline de Soie* trimmed with Valenciennes lace which she specially requested to be simple. Grandmother Locoul would have sent the most handsome silks and laces or satin, had she been allowed to do so.

Désirée Archinard's engagement fan 1857

But, Mother wanted only a simple ceremony, on account of her mother's illness. Céphalide was brought in seated in a rolling chair so that she might witness the ceremony, which made her very happy. The farewells on the next day were very sad, for Mother feared she might never see her own mother again.

But, with promises of meeting soon again, Mother was sustained for the day. On the boat trip down the Mississippi, they stopped at the plantation to see Grandmother Elisabeth Locoul before they proceeded to New Orleans.

Barely a week had elapsed when Mother had a dream that her mother was dying and calling for her. Mother was so dreadfully disturbed by this. The next night, Father awakened her as she sobbed in her sleep. Mother said she had seen her mother dead and knew where she lay, and what she wore and that she even saw the silver coins placed on her eyes to close her lids. Mother could not be comforted, for she knew the details were too realistic and that the end had come.

Alas! In those days, news was so slow to reach, no telegraph, and letters were landed from a boat with very long fishing poles and rushed by negroes or anyone who would deliver them. She wrote at once to Grandfather Phanor Prud'Homme telling him of her dreams and told the hour and the night she had dreamed these details.

It had happened just as Mother had seen it and, yes, her mother had been buried five days before the news reached her. Mother's grief was so great that Father took her from the plantation to New Orleans and, before she knew it, they were on a vessel bound for Europe where they spent many months traveling.

My father's sister, Aimée, the *Madame* de Lobel-Mahy, had a large town house in the Faubourg St. Germain in Paris where they spent the summer. Aunt Aimée insisted that Father and Mother should occupy her apartment where she had a splendid *"bonne à tout faire,"* a servant who looked after the apartment. They did so against Mother's wishes, who preferred to be at the hotel, the whole time fearing to hurt my aunt's feelings if they refused.

My parents made frequent visits to the large house near the Tuilleries where the de Lobels lived in expensive high style, as my Uncle Ivan de Lobel was spending his wife's money very generously and entertained all (as Father called them) his "broken down, titled relations." Mother particularly noticed the faded silks they wore and the second- or third-class coaches they always took instead of first-class passage. The de Lobel-Mahys had three children: Eugénie, Raymond and Fanny, all three born in Europe.

The trip was most beneficial to Mother. When they left Paris and bade farewell to everyone, Julie, their very efficient French maid at the apartment, wept pitifully. Julie had never known, she said, "such good and generous people as the Americans." Mother had found her crying once for her little child who she had to board elsewhere and who was suffering for want of clothes. So, Mother went to the stores and had sent up every possible thing a child could need for warmth and comfort. Julie had nearly passed out with gratitude. But, when Father gave her a nice little sum of money besides her wages, she was speechless and the tears flowed as she kissed their hands. As they left, Julie showered blessings upon them, saying she always wanted to work for Americans, as they had such generous hearts.

Mother was in such better spirits upon her return, and much stronger. Unfortunately, she was to experience, in the next few years, the loss of three children, prematurely born. And, when I announced myself, she was compelled to remain quiet on her couch for nine months, so as to prevent any accident, if possible. But, I had come to stay and I had my destiny to fulfill.

THE CIVIL WAR AND AFTER

The Civil War between the North and the South had broken out on April, 1861, and I was born in December of the same year. My mother knew all this time that Father would have to go to the front as soon as we were both safe enough to be left behind. She worried terribly about it. I am sure that all this brooding had its effect upon my nervous system, for I have always worried, all my life.

Emile Locoul

My father, having had military training in his youth, summoned all the eligible Acadians of St. James Parish and they rallied to his call. He drilled them and equipped them at his own expense and then, he led them to the front. *"Les Gardes de St. Jacques,"* the Guards of St. James Parish, with Captain Locoul at their head, did splendid work and stood the privations and hardships of the Confederate Army marvelously. They worshiped my father and his word with them was law. Colonel Gustave Breaux once said jokingly to my father, "Those damn Acadians of yours would have run me through if I had not given the password, even knowing who I was, because *le Capitaine Locoul a dit de ne pas laisser passer personne sans le mot d'ordre,"* because "Captain Locoul said not to let anyone pass without the password."

Fearing that gunboats would soon run up the River and shell the plantation, Father obtained a furlough of a few days so that he could come to St. James to drive us to the northern part of the State. Before he could reach the plantation, the Union gunboats came upriver, bombing. With the gunboat approaching, Mother escaped with me in a buggy, wrapping me up in a tablecloth with the silverware.

Odiot silver tray
upon which Laura was placed in the 1862 escape from the Duparc & Locoul Plantation. Initials at top of tray read: "LDD" for original owner, Louis de Mézière Duparc

We found out later that, immediately after we left the plantation, Grandmother Locoul had traveled with the de Lobels to central Louisiana, far from the gunboats that might come up the Mississippi River and shell the Locoul Plantation. As was feared, the place was shelled, four cannonballs hitting the big house. All the windows, glass and china were shattered. All that was saved was Mother's lovely china creamer and an unmatching silver square sugarbowl.

We were met by Father on the way and went as far as New Iberia at Dr. DuPerier's, who was an old friend of Father's. Father left us there until step-Grandfather Phanor Prud'Homme could come for us and take us to Natchitoches. The DuPeriers were adorable to Mother and me and did all in their power to make her happy and comfortable with her baby.

Incidentally, Mrs. DuPerier was the sole survivor of her entire family during the tragedy of Last Island on the Gulf Coast of Louisiana. The story of Last Island has been written by Lafcadio Hearn under the name of <u>Chita</u> and he received much of his information from Mrs. Rob Naquin who had lost every member of her family there except for one brother who was away at college.

A tidal wave washed away nearly all the guests at this summer resort. Mrs. DuPerier was picked up, unconscious, floating on a branch and the young doctor who nursed the patients who were on the rescue boat, took her to his mother's home once he realized that she had lost every member of her family. Several months later, when an uncle came to her, it was too late. She had lost her heart to the young doctor and he to her, and they were married. But, Mrs. DuPerier could never hear the howling of the winds without rushing to her room and closing the door in panic.

Accompanying us on this escape trip to Natchitoches and New Iberia was Louise, or just, "Mammie," as we always called her. Mammie was Mother's slave and had come to the Locoul Plantation in St. James with Mother when she married Father in 1857. But, when I was born, a nurse was needed for me and another slave was obtained in a very fortunate way.

While Mother was rocking me to sleep one day at the Locoul Plantation, she heard Grandmother Locoul bargaining on the back gallery with a negro slave trader who was on horseback. Poor Anna, the slave girl, was there with her young child, Toussaint, in her arms and weeping bitterly. Mother, who could see what was unfolding, realized at once the cause of Anna's cries. Mother called for Father hastily to come to her, telling him, "I believe your mother is selling Anna and separating her from her child. Wouldn't that be the same as if our baby were taken from us?"

Slave Cabins,
Laura Plantation,
built in the 1840s

32

Fired with paternal feelings, Father walked up to the man, taking no notice of his mother, and said, "I don't know what transaction my mother made with you, but, if she wants to sell this woman, my money is as good as yours, and I will buy her. Otherwise, you may depart at once." Grandmother Elisabeth was furious at his interference, saying that Father and Mother spoiled every servant they had and were *"des gateurs des nègres"* or "negro spoilers."

Poor, dear Anna was eventually turned over to Mother. Anna never forgot the incident that had saved her child and worshiped the ground my father and mother walked on. Anna was to be my nurse and lived with us until I married and left New Orleans in 1892. As a child, I loved to sit in her lap and listen to all the funny stories she told me about the family. She came from Wilmington, North Carolina and the Creole negro servants hated the American negroes and made them very unhappy because they did not speak the negro French dialect.

Father had a devoted servant and valet, Lucien, who followed him all through the War, saving his life on several occasions. Once, as Father lay under a tree, burning up with fever, Lucien heard the galloping of horses and knew they were Yankees. If that were so, Father would be taken prisoner. So, hastily grabbing Father in his arms, he helped him to his saddle, saying, *"Monsieur* Locoul, hold on to the pummel. The Yankees are coming." Lucien took hold of the bridle and galloped off until he reached the Confederate lines and safety. There, he nursed my father until he was well.

"Millie Anne,"
former slave at Riverlake
Plantation

Although Father was an unusually strong and healthy man, the hardships of the War and a fare of salt pork and cornbread helped to undermine his constitution, accustomed to the luxuries of life and his bottle of Bordeaux claret at every meal. Lucien was a fine cook and prepared things whenever he could get them for Father. He also washed and looked after Father's clothes, besides caring for three horses and buggy that Father had with him. The three were a white riding horse, "Bismarque," and a pair of beautiful, matched black ones called "Byron" and "Lamartine."

33

Mother often told me of an occasion during the War when I was nearly dying of whooping cough at the Prud'Homme's and had to be taken to the town of Natchitoches immediately for treatment. Father drove her, with an almost dying child in her arms, and was fairly burning up the ground to get to town, when some drunken Yankee soldiers lumbered up and rode beside us, screaming and swearing and yelling, disregarding Father's pleas to let him pass with his sick child. Mother, knowing that Father might lose his temper, stole his pistol away from him.

At that point, the horses took fright and darted, headlong, the reins stretching out tight in Father's hands. He held the reins, trying to hold the horses in. Lucien, who was following behind on horseback, immediately realized that a real tragedy was about to happen. He had to stop them before they reached a sharp turn in the way a mile further. Lucien broke the branch of a small tree and dashed ahead alongside of the runaway team, calling the horses by name, speaking to them and trying to stroke their heads gently. Just before we reached the levee where it turns, Father had them under control. We entered the town and I was saved.

By the end of the third year of the War, the brave Acadians became homesick and disheartened. The hardships of war were telling on them and they yearned for their families and homes. Taking to the high woods, they gradually got back to St. James Parish as best they could. Father then reported to Colonel Breaux and joined the quartermaster department, until the end of the War.

When Robt. E. Lee had been forced to surrender and the Southern Cause was lost, Father returned to Natchitoches and remained at Grandfather Phanor Prud'homme's home. It was months before that his second child was born: George Locoul, who came on the 2nd of September, 1864.

My very first recollection is of the day we left Natchitoches to make our home at Grandmother Locoul's plantation in St. James Parish. I remember Grandfather Phanor hugging and squeezing me with all his heart, my Aunt Irène, broken-hearted to part with my mother, and the little sternwheel boat loaded to the brim with cotton bales that we embarked upon for our trip down the river.

View of the River
at Baton Rouge
from
"Ballou's Pictorial"

We went to New Orleans first, as Father wished to find out what he had left from the bank. A friend of Father's, a Mr. Stephen Gaudet, who was the teller at the old Citizen's Bank, had written after Father's name on the books: *"Emile Locoul, when last heard of, gone to Europe."* And, by this statement, was saved all the money Father had left in the bank. It was only $2,000 which the Union General Butler did not confiscate as he did from all those who went to war on the southern side.

Grandmother Locoul's house at 101 Toulouse Street, just in back of the Opera House, was left by the Yankees, who took possession of it, in a state of horror, desecration and filth beyond description. Strange as it seems, though, Mother's rooms on the 3rd floor, with her beautiful rosewood carved furniture, was left in fairly good condition. Mother always attributed it to the fact that she had a little old-fashioned sheep-skin trunk that was covered with all the paraphernalia of a "high mason." This covering belonged to her father, François Archinard, and the Yankees took it with them. But, believing the contents of the trunk to belong to the owner of the room, they respected the rest of the furniture and furnishings.

Father, with his two thousand dollars, equipped the family with clothes, gave Mother a carriage and a pair of horses, got himself a new gun, and we went to the plantation to live with Grandmother Locoul in the big family home. Aunt Aimée and Uncle Ivan de Lobel, who had come from Europe during the War, lived with Grandmother and made their home in another house across the yard, and Grandmother catered for the two families.

Manor House
Duparc & Locoul
Plantation
1870s

At the end of the War, both our families returned to the plantation, which had not been devastated as many others had been. Where most of the other planters had suffered great losses and many had lost their plantations, the Duparc and Locoul Plantation had not been hurt in any way.

The Civil War came and the Civil War left, and nothing changed on the place. The work went on as usual. The old, former slaves remained on the place and, for several years, three years to be exact, there was a profit of $75,000 after the sugar making was over. We children never knew what privation or want meant after the War, as so many did. Everything was plentiful, servants to do every service, and we had our horses, dogs and pets and enjoyed life as children who do not know care.

Even at an early age I can remember how different it all seemed, coming from a home where I was loved and petted and spoiled, to one where we felt as strangers, unloved and unfriendly. Grandmother Locoul was not demonstrative, not the loving grandmother we always heard about. She favored her daughter's children and gave them all her love.

It was no secret that Father's marriage was a great disappointment to them all. My father had waited so long to marry and they hoped, for their own inheritance sake, that he would remain a bachelor. But, when he did marry, and I finally came to stay, they felt cheated out of an inheritance which they might have had.

I remember walking with my nurse in the yard at the plantation, holding "Buddy" (my little brother, George) by the hand and seeing for the first time, my three cousins: Eugénie, Raymond and Fannie (who was two years older than I). Our nurse told Mother afterwards that they whispered to each other, *"Voilà, les petits voleurs qui viennent voler l'héritage de Mantoul,"* as they called Grandmother. In other words, "Here are the little robbers who have come to steal Grandmother's inheritance." However, in times to come, we became very friendly, even if our parents were not. For my father and his brother-in-law, Ivan de Lobel, could never have been friends. Father was the soul of honor, justice and integrity, and these traits were unknown to his brother-in-law.

"The little robbers,"
George (left) &
Laura Locoul
1866

My Uncle Ivan de Lobel-Mahy was not happy to be in America and only awaited the death of his mother-in-law, so that he might inherit the Locoul wealth and then return with his family to his cherished France. This was a joy he was never to know, as he survived Grandmother Locoul by only a few months and died in New Orleans.

37

Children of our age are very adaptable, and it was not long before we began to feel at home, getting into everything and being on the spot whenever anything was taking place. When the time came for shearing the sheep, I was there to watch them do it. Or, when hogs were killed in the winter for the lard and sausages, blood puddings, cracklins and hogshead cheese, I would be there to see it all. I always wanted the hog's bladder for they were cured in some way and then dried, softened and used for the inside of tobacco pouches, made of silks and embroidery and a draw-string with small tassels at the top, which I made for father's tobacco and gave him on his birthday or on Christmas.

The most exciting day was when they branded the young cattle. I was up and dressed very early and ran to the cattle lot. But, when I saw them take the red-hot iron from the fire to brand the young calves or cows, I would stop up my ears, turn my back and run, only to return to do the same thing all over again until the branding was done. It was so cruel that I shivered whenever I thought of it, but, there was a greater shock in store for me yet.

One day as I stood on the top of the well where water was pumped into a long trough for the horses and cattle to drink, a weather-beaten old negro named Pa Philippe, whose work it was to pump the water, was standing close to me. On his creased and wrinkled old face I saw the letters "V.D.P." I pointed my finger to

Slave quarters
Riverlake Plantation

his face and asked, "Oh, Pa Philippe, what is that mark on your forehead?" He turned to me and laughed in a hard, cackling, old voice saying, "Lord, child, don't you know this is where they branded me when I used to run away?"

I was horror stricken and ran into the house to my mother, saying, "Oh, Mamma, they branded Pa Philippe like they do the cattle. I saw it. He told me so. Who did it, Mamma? Who did it?" She gathered me into her arms and hugged me, saying, "My dear child, I had hoped you would never hear of these cruelties until you were much older and I am very sorry Philippe told you about it." Then she tried, as best she could, to explain how there are people on the plantation who would never do this and that there are people whom I know and love who have done horrible things. It all made a lasting impression on me and I always wanted to be kind to Pa Philippe after that. I often took cake and other things from the table to him.

Pa Philippe must have been hard to manage in his early years because Grandmother Locoul never had a kind word for him and, when he would pass in the yard, driving the cattle, she hurled epithets at him which no one but herself could say as fast and with as much meaning. Her pet expressions were: *"coquin, canaille, voleur and pichon,"* all screaming, more or less, degrees of "thief."

Copy of Runaway advertisement in the Louisiana Courier newspaper, 1816

Runaway Slaves.

Ranaway from the Duparc plantation on the 27th ult. and the 2d last, six *American* negroes, not speaking a word of French. The named **SAM** is of the age of about 22 years, of the height of 5 feet 6, in French measure, has a reddish complexion and stout make; the second named **PETER** of about the same age, of the height of 5 feet 2 in, of a dark complexion, and having some white spots on his lips, his legs some what crooked, very strong and robust; the third named **RESIDENCE** of the age of about 21 years, of the height of 5 feet 5 in, a dark complexion and slender body; the 4th named **THOMAS** is of the age of 27 years, of the height of 5 feet 7 in, stout build and very big, has a very dark complexion, a scar on one of his cheeks, and a very thick beard; the 5th named **JOSEPH** (or **JOE**) is of the age of 17 years, of the height of 5 feet 2 in, has a dark complexion, a face somewhat swelled, small and hollow eyes and slender body. The sixth named **PHILIP** is of the age 20 years, of the height of 5 feet 6 in, slender body and red skin. He is branded on the two cheeks V.D.P. (for the Widow Duparc PrudHomme), the latter slave was purchased from Mr. John Cox; the five others bought from Mr. Robert Thompson now in this city.

A reward of 200 dollars will be paid to whomever shall lodge the said slaves in any of the jails of this state, or bring them back to their master on the Duparc plantation, in the county of Acadia. Thirty dollars will be given for each of them in case they should not be stopped altogether. All reasonable charges will besides be paid for by:

Louis Dre. Duparc   December 6, 1816

Armant Plantation
manor house,
built ca. 1805,
now demolished

One of the few persons who ever visited Grandmother Locoul was a Miss Aglaë Armant, our neighbor from the plantation just upriver from us. Miss Aglaë called her, *"Marraine"* because Grandmother was her God-Mother. She was a small, white-haired, little lady, who, every Sunday, taught the little negroes their Catechism and, in the winter, she taught school in her home to the Acadian children who lived in the village.

Every Sunday afternoon Grandmother would send for her. She lived with her brother who owned the village store. The two ladies would talk for hours in Grandmother's parlor in the winter, and on the porch in the summer.

Later on, Miss Aglaë got a little surrey that looked like a chicken box on wheels and she had a negro boy drive her. Visitors always had a driver and a little negro boy sitting in front to get down and run to open the gates and close them again.

Miss Aglaë was devoted to my mother and, some years later, Mother was called when Miss Aglaë was ill and died. Mother directed the carpenter in making of the coffin, as the dead had to be buried the next day. Mother helped him cover the outside with black fabric, putting silver-headed tacks on top in the form of a cross. They had my brother, George, bring a two-mule wagon to drive to the burial grounds of the parish church of St. James which was ten miles away, some distance in those days. When they put the body of Miss Aglaë into the coffin, she was far too small for it, so George got one pillow and then another to stuff in the sides so she would not be jolted around.

Mother said that Miss Aglaë was the only person ever to have left her anything in a will. In her living room were two plain but handsome rockers with gracefully carved mahogany sides. These she willed to Mother; her other possessions going to other friends.

Her will was found, neither signed nor dated, so her relatives in New Orleans who paid no attention to her got what little she left.

Before her death, Miss Aglaë had a cousin from New Orleans who came to visit her for three or four months, a Mr. Armant. He spent much time at our plantation and was very devoted to me. Mr. Armant was the head of a group of military men and they attended the Military Mass that was held every year at the old St. Louis Cathedral.

During Mass, the sexton would walk down the aisle knocking his long stick with a large pear-shaped silver top. Boom, Boom! it sounded as he went along. But, all the military men stayed in the back of the church. Mr. Armant was the one to pass the collection basket around. Actually, he would ask his lady friend to walk with him. She would hold on to his arm with one hand and hold the basket with the other, everyone putting in dollar bills, as they were too ashamed to put less with the lady collecting. I often asked him if he had asked his lady friend to pass the basket with him and he would answer, "Only in your absence, Miss Laura."

Parish Church of St. James Cabahanoce

IN SICKNESS AND IN HEALTH

I had learned to ride horseback on the mare named "Lucy" which was left for the children, for she was so gentle. And, once or twice, when I fell off, she spread her legs and stood quietly until I was rescued. Then, later, we had our own ponies, as Father was very fond of horses and he raised them for the pleasure of racing them. He often said they had a strain of Arabian in them. Father had a ledger book in which he kept the age and pedigree of his horses. He had bought a magnificent stallion called "Van Dyke" who was taken care of by a special negro servant who took him out each day to pasture, rub tonic on him and feed him.

Old horse barn
Laura Plantation

One thing that frequently used to provoke me so much was, during the year, I was told not to go out of the fenced yard around the house but, instead, to practice my piano, to read a book or to do something I didn't want to do. But George, my little brother, was allowed to go out. And then, suddenly, he would come bursting into the house, all excitement, to make the announcement that there was a little, new colt in the yard, or a new calf. Only then was I permitted to go out and see the new arrival.

In the yard were any number of large pecan trees which were thrashed every other year. A negro who was expert in climbing trees used a long bamboo cane, or "wild cane" as we called them. He would, first, thrash the upper-most branches, descending gradually to the lower branches. As the pecans fell to the ground, they were picked up by a dozen or more little negro children from the worker's quarters. As they gathered them, they were emptied into a barrel under the tree. When these barrels were filled, they were shipped to New Orleans and sold. I have seen as many as twelve or thirteen barrels filled at a time.

The proceeds of the gathering were given by Grandmother Locoul to her six grandchildren at Christmas: to the three de Lobels and ourselves. The negro children hired for the purpose of gathering the pecans were paid at the end of that day with a tin can of nuts.

It was on one of these pecan thrashing days, one bright October day in 1868 that I was sent out of the house to pick pecans with the other children and kept out of the house. I felt that all was not well and wanted to be with my mother. But, the nurse always found some excuse to keep me away and I was very unhappy. That night at eight o'clock, my father came for me in great glee, telling me that I had a little sister and took me in to see her. But, I ran to my mother's arms and could not be dragged away until she comforted me and made me promise to take care of my little brother, George, until she was well again.

Former slaves on the plantation 1880s

Every evening, huge pails of milk were brought in and poured into large yellow bowls and allowed to clabber. The next morning, the cream was skimmed off to make butter. It had been the custom since slavery to give the negroes the surplus milk and clabber every morning. A stream of negro children came with their tin pans from the quarters for the clabber. A large table had stood under the back of the house for that purpose and the dining-room girl dished out the clabber to them. Then the cream was put in a tall, old-fashioned wooden churn. I loved to be allowed to take the handle and jump as I churned, singing, "Come, come, come butter, come." But, I didn't like the home-made butter and always wanted the yellow, rancid butter from the country store.

The old, deserted slave hospital stood in the yard near the quarters and had not been used since the War, but there was something very spooky and mysterious looking about it. We liked to go there with our nurse, creep up the steps slowly and walk around on tiptoe until we heard noises, or imagining we did. Then, we would tear down the steps as fast as we could go. I was told about the "stock" where the negroes were put when they ran away, but I was only eight years old and very small.

On special occasions the negroes asked permission to use the hospital for parties or weddings and Mother furnished the candles and gave them coffee and the ingredients for cakes. The negroes loved Mother and always came to her when in trouble, or when they were sick, for medicines. I have seen her many times, in the middle of the night, go with one or two negroes, one respectfully holding her arm while the other walked ahead with a lantern, to their cabin to see an ill wife or child.

There was only one country doctor for miles around and, when anyone was sick in the big house or in the quarters, a pole with a white towel tacked to it was placed in the front gate to notify the doctor as he passed that he was wanted.

So as to insure the doctor of a certain income each year, each family paid him five dollars a head, and each negro, one dollar per head per year. The planters always presented the doctor with his sugar supply, molasses, rice, etc., etc. for the year.

Pantry Room in the Manor House
Laura Plantation

Big blisters seemed to be the great remedy of the day. A piece of yellow adhesive cloth made for the purpose was cut about three inches wide, a black paste of something was thickly smeared over it and then washed with "Cantharadine," a powder made from some insect which was placed on any part of the body. This raised huge blisters which was supposed to relieve inflammation. When the old blister was removed, the wound was dressed with pieces of young banana leaves, spread with olive oil and repeated for several days till the place had healed. The pantry shelves in the house still contained bottles of every kind of medicine. When I was older, I was allowed to weigh the quinine in the scales and to wrap it in small packages of paper.

When the cholera raged one summer and negroes were dropping in the fields, they were brought to their cabins to die. George and I watched all this by climbing into an old apple tree to munch green apples or persimmons or anything that came our way. Mother was too busy looking after the sick and thought we were safe at play. There were frequent outbreaks of cholera and yellow fever and I now often wonder how we ever escaped. But, we were the sturdiest bunch of roughnecks that anybody seemed to know.

On another occasion in the middle of the night, I heard someone call and tell Mother that the overseer's old mother was dying and, please, to come over at once. This seemed to be an opportunity I could not miss! I rushed to the overseer's house across the yard and entered the bedroom on tip-toe, for all the family were on their knees, weeping. Mother was wiping the forehead of the woman and reading the litany of the dying and I stood peering over the foot of the bed.

Then the poor, old lady gave one last dying gasp and with it, she spit out stuff from her mouth called the "black vomit," the surest thing of yellow fever. Some of the vomit splashed on me and Mother, in the midst of her prayers, glanced up and saw me! Well, down went the prayer book. Mother tore after me and I slid down the steps until I was caught by someone before I got to my house.

Poor Mother was horrified! I was rushed to the wash house, a small building in the yard, washed, bathed and dressed in fresh clothes while my old clothes remained to be disinfected before I returned to the house.

Later, my cousin, Céline, who lived with us, caught the disease, a bad case. Mother housed her with an old nanny without a doctor, as he could not find the time to get around. Mother was able to find some ice for Céline. Ice was so necessary and only small pieces could be obtained at any time and it had to be wrapped in sand and a piece of carpet. It was impossible to separate Céline and me and Providence watched over us.

Planters House & Sugar Plantation
on the Mississippi River
Gleason's Pictorial

SCHOOL LIFE BEGINS

When I was seven years old, Miss Ellen Pooley came to be governess to my three cousins and she lived in the big house with us. She was engaged to teach me, also, and, immediately after breakfast, I had my lessons until ten o'clock. Then, she went over to the other house across the yard to teach the de Lobels until three o'clock.

My Tante Aimée de Lobel spared no effort for the education of her three children and turned her parlor into a study room during the day. An old French professor, Monsieur Medout, who lived on the de Lobel's small plantation, "Lobelia," located several miles downriver, came every morning on horseback to teach them French.

Laura Locoul
11 years old

On Lobelia was a nice, little house, kept up by a woman who was a splendid cook and the de Lobels entertained friends from New Orleans there and friends of the children were also invited. Uncle Ivan de Lobel had a large cage on the gallery where he kept reptiles and rattlesnakes, the most poisonous snake in this country.

Mrs. Choppin, a neighbor living ten miles upriver, had a young governess, Miss Jeannie Prentice, who taught music, also, and, every Saturday, my cousins were taken there to take music lessons from her. I frequently met with them for the ride back in the big black omnibus that we called "Black Maria" which Grandmother Locoul had gotten for them.

Miss Pooley held her classes in the afternoon and practicing was done in-between times. Miss Pooley lived with us for three years and then left at the death of her sister whose children needed her care. Mother considered her a wonderful teacher and often regretted she had not been with us longer to give me a better start.

OUR OWN HOME ON BOURBON STREET

In the meantime, Mother's long dream of happiness had come true. Father had bought a home for her in New Orleans at 35 Bourbon Street, one block and a half from Canal Street and within a short distance of the old Opera House. We sang and spoke of nothing else and Mother was too happy for it to last.

Rosewood
"Duchesse"
Emile bought for
Désirée's
bedroom suite

We went down to New Orleans to furnish the house and Father wanted only the best of everything. Mother would restrain him, saying, "The simpler things will do now. Wait until Laura is about eighteen and comes out." Alas! How little the dreamer knew, how different the experience and the world would be when Laura was eighteen.

On several occasions, Father did as he wanted to and, among many handsome things he had sent us, were the two large French mirrors which rested on the mantelpieces of the double-arch parlors, imported by Mallard, an old importer of French furniture.

My Aunt Irène, Mother's only sister, whom she had not seen for ten years or more, was coming to spend the winter with us with her two happy children. I had never seen Mother more radiantly happy. We were going to go to the school in the City, George and I, and everything seemed to be coming our way.

Barely one month later, we received a letter from Natchitoches stating that Aunt Irène had died there. In the music of happy preparations for the joyful reunion they both so longed for, it was a bitter blow from which Mother did not recover for a long time, especially as she knew her sister was unhappily married and did not know how the children would be cared for. This certainly threw a damper on the happiness of being in our own home. But, we spent the winter at our new home for the "Season" and Mother and I loved it immensely.

Bourbon Street
1868
from
Frank Leslie's
Illustrated
Newspaper

THE LAURA PLANTATION

Finally, in the spring, Grandmother Locoul made the grand announcement that she had decided to divide the plantation in half between her two children, a thing she should have done ten years earlier.

*Elisabeth Locoul
née Duparc*

Grandmother was a very bright woman, but strong-willed. She had never wanted to give up the reins of government and, now, she was nearing 80 years of age. The place had been so terribly neglected and allowed to deteriorate. No new improvements had been made and, when she decided to divide the plantation, it meant ruin to both her children for it was too late.

Louisiana Sugarmill from "Harper's Weekly"

After Grandmother's announcement there followed one long year of misery before things were settled. My father was given the choice of sides, being the older of the two children. But, whenever he made a decision, Grandmother, after interviewing her son-in-law and daughter, would decree that certain buildings would be removed to the other side and make so many such changes that it was all off again. Arguments by the hour, unpleasant feelings and harsh words ensued. The subject would be dropped to begin all over again.

At last, Father chose the downriver side with the large homestead, the overseer's house, the stables and part of the negro quarters. The upriver side had the family sugarmill, negro quarters, the hospital and several outer buildings. A certain sum of money ($10,000) was to go to the one without the mill so as to build one. The main sugarmill was to be used by both until that was done.

Désirée Archinard
&
Emile Locoul

That first year, things went smoothly throughout, for there was not much cane to grind. Father, had kept most of his cane back for a large crop for the next year. Prospects seemed very good, and we were all very hopeful when the bomb exploded in our midst.

My grandmother, who was always the intermediary, came, after many sighs, hemming and hawing and many brisk walks up and down the broad gallery, and told Father that Mr. de Lobel had decided that his crop could not be ground in the same sugarmill as it made too much confusion. This was the beginning of September and the cane must be ground before December, as the cold weather freezes cane and frozen cane cannot be turned into sugar.

Loading cane
at the sugarmill,
from
"Harper's Weekly"

Father was frantic. How a murder was not committed on the place, nor a duel fought, is only due to my blessed mother's wonderful diplomacy. Father swore that, "I will let every darn cane rot in the ground." There really did not seem much else to do.

The news soon spread and, from a clear sky, Mr. LeGendre, whose place was three miles downriver, came to see Father and insisted that he leave by the next train and get the Texas & Pacific Railroad to lend him a number of boxcars that could be filled with cane between regular train hours. The plan was that the cane would be pushed in the available cars along the track by the negroes to Mr. LeGendre's place and then grind it there.

Each week they should be able to cut and move enough cane for one full grinding, but, only if the whole force of workmen were thrown into the job. Not once did I ever doubt that Mother was at the bottom of this as she and Mrs. LeGendre were close friends. Father finally consented, secured the boxcars and the weeks of "pilgrim's progress" began.

Crushing cane
from
"Harper's
Weekly"
1883

October turned out to be a very cold initiation to winter. The poor negroes were Devotion itself to Father, and did their utmost to save the crop, working with legs wrapped in gunnysacks and hands almost frozen from hauling cane that was covered with ice.

Only one half of the crop was saved and the rest of the cane had to be hauled and dumped into the marshes. This meant ruin and Father, who had just suffered his first attack of gout, was frightfully dismayed. All the while, my dear, little mother fought for her children unceasingly, boosting Father, cheering him and urging him on to better luck.

After the War, many planters had started an economical way of working on shares with the negroes. Mother secured one of their contracts, read it to the negroes on our place and made them go in a body and ask Father to let them work on shares. They were to be furnished with their provisions during the year, which was deducted at the end of the year from their shares. The workers did as Mother had asked. Father, not knowing the instigator back of this plan, was touched by their desire to help him and, while "the iron was hot," the contracts were signed and, for two years, the place was worked in this way.

Inside a sugarmill
from
"Harper's Weekly"
1883

So, the new sugarhouse was to be built. Father chose the old builder, Tassin, who had put up every building on the place, including the big sugarhouse on the other side, which cost nearly $10,000. Everyone thought he was a good choice.

Just as the mill was nearing completion, the old man, who had married a young wife, absconded with the money that was given him, including cash and salaries set aside for the workmen, and he left the State.

However, the sugarhouse was finished in time for the grinding season by Mr. Tassin's assistant, who had been duped, as well. So, the canes were ground, no incidents occurred (which was due, I am sure, to the number of Miraculous Medals that Mother had placed herself between the masonry as the walls went up). Not much profit was made, for the loss of the last few years had been so great.

At the ending of grinding season, a number of neighbors came to celebrate and christen the new sugarhouse. Among them was my friend, Lily LeGendre. She brought a huge stalk of sugarcane, with a blue ribbon tied to it, with "THE LAURA" marked in gold letters, and presented it to Father, and the mill and the plantation were then christened "**THE LAURA**" for me. Later, the mark for the sugar sold from the plantation would be a large gold crescent moon with "LAURA" written within it and, I am told, to this day, the plantation still bears my name.

Of course, we now lived on the plantation entirely. Father, along with the overseer, looked after the place and Mother renewed her energy in trying to make the old place into a real home. For eight years during this time, Father represented the Parish of St. James in the Louisiana Legislature. Grandmother Locoul spent the winters in her own home in New Orleans with her daughter and her family and she spent her summers with us. We had to have a governess again and Mother secured the services of Miss Rhoda Tucker, whose father was a friend of my father's when they had been in the Legislature together and she came to us very highly recommended by Miss Ellen Pooley, our former governess.

THE DUEL

Miss Tucker's arrival on the plantation could never have been more ill-timed for a stranger than when she came. The whole place was in a tumult of excitement. Father was in New Orleans on business, Mother was nearly wild and we children were just as excited, not knowing what it meant or what it was all about.

Fannie de Lobel

A duel was to take place the next day between my Uncle Ivan de Lobel and our overseer, Mr. Arnold LeBourgeois. The overseer on our place was a gentleman and sincere, and related to several owners of large plantations by the same name. Fortune had not favored him. He had a large family and had become on overseer to support his family. We children were delighted to have others of our own age to play with and, at once, became very friendly. My cousin, Fannie de Lobel, the youngest of her family and two years older than I, was frequently with us and began a very mild flirtation with one of the older sons, Louis Alcée LeBourgeois, who was studying to become a builder and, he was quite good looking.

It chanced to pass one day that as Fannie stood on the front gallery of the old hospital that had been converted into their very comfortable home, she waved her handkerchief to Louis Alcée who was crossing the yard on our side of the place.

Fannie's father, Ivan de Lobel, who was leaving the house, saw her and his fury was uncontrollable for such a calm man! That his daughter should dare look at an overseer's son was too much for him to bear. So, he immediately wrote to Mr. LeBourgeois asking him to send his son away and demanding that he not set foot on his side of the place, in reparation of his wounded feelings. In part, Uncle Ivan's note said, *"Il vous a plu de faire de votre fils un vilain charpentier, vous n'avez pas le droit de regarder si haut,"* that is, "It has pleased you to make of your son a degenerate carpenter. You have no right to aspire so high."

Mr. LeBourgeois read the note and immediately came over to see Mother, who had been watching from every angle of the house. He showed her my uncle's note and his reply, which said that he would not send his son away and that he considered that Mr. de Lobel was asking very little, indeed, in reparation of his wounded feelings, not to have Louis Alcée set foot on his half of the plantation. Mother raised her hands in horror and screamed, "Mr. LeBourgeois, do you realize what your are sending? *C'est une carte!* It is a challenge!" "I know, Madam," he replied, "but I take an insult from no man. He then sent the note over by our yardboy.

Shortly afterwards, we saw my uncle and his valet drive off in his buggy and, a few hours later, Uncle Ivan returned with his two friends as witnesses, Colonel Roman and *Monsieur* de Longpré. Colonel Roman then took the challenge to Mr. LeBourgeois, who accepted it. And having the choice of weapons, Mr. LeBourgeois chose the double-barreled shotgun at 40 paces. Mr. LeBourgeois sent for two of his friends as witnesses. By evening, the duel was set for noon the next day on a far off knoll on the place called "Buzzard's Roost."

Grandmother walked up and down the gallery abusing Mr. LeBourgeois. Mother was hoping and praying that Father would return the next day, and the poor stranger, Mrs. Tucker, after being told the facts, locked herself in her room and kept to herself.

The next morning, I scrambled into the buggy that went to the train station to wait and pick up poor, dear Daddy. He was so unsuspecting of trouble, and was returning from the City, laden down with packages of fruit and candy for us, and with grouse for Mother. He had barely taken his seat in the buggy when George and I almost crawled over him, talking at the same time, trying to tell him of the excitement. When we reached the house, Mother received him shouting, but he put his arm around her and pulled her into the room, saying, "What the devil are Laura and George trying to tell me? What has happened?"

Mother then had to explain. She had barely finished when Aunt Aimée de Lobel came running over, saying, "Emile, *mon cher frère*, can't you stop this duel? Ivan will be killed!" Aunt Aimée wept bitterly and assured Father that he could and must stop what was about to happen.

Father could not see how in the world he could stop it, as it had gone so far and he knew none of the details. Then, one after another of his friends dropped in with the same urgent requests and, in despair, Father said, "Let the witnesses on both sides come to my room and I will see what I can do."

Dueling under the oaks in New Orleans, from "Harper's Weekly" 1866

In the meantime, the two doctors had arrived and were in readiness, both parties were dressed in white and the carriages were waiting to take the duelists to the fighting grounds. Mr. LeBourgeois' young children were sobbing at his side, and, on the other side, the de Lobels were in deepest despair because Mr. LeBourgeois had fought in two duels previously and wounded his adversaries both times. While my uncle Ivan was not at all familiar with the shotgun, he was an expert swordsman.

In less than one half-hour, a meeting took place and, after much discussion, they asked Father to sign a paper saying that if he had been here and had asked Mr. LeBourgeois to send his son away, that he is sure he would have done it. The two men recanted their absurd statements and that seemed to be quite satisfactory to the witnesses (all were fathers of families), and all of whom wanted to avert the duel at any cost.

Due honor on both sides was satisfied and gradually the tension grew less and turned to jollification. Father and Uncle de Lobel had not been on speaking terms since the episode of the sugar-house. That evening, I was in the yard when *Tante* Aimée came running and caught me by the arm, saying, *"Ou es ton Père? Va, le chercher et amene le toute suite"* or "Where is your father? Go, find him and bring him here immediately." I found Father and then delivered the message. He was so terribly disgruntled, saying, "I have done what they wanted. Why don't they leave me alone?"

But, *Tante* Aimée had reached us by then and had Father by the arm, bringing him to the dividing line between our places where the others awaited. Father reached the border line and stood firmly, stopping short on his side. From there he would not move another step. *Tante* Aimée saw him standing still and called out, "Messieurs." Then my Uncle de Lobel walked forward, extending his hand, saying, *"Locoul, permettez moi de vous serrer la main, vous m'avez sauvé la vie,"* or "Locoul, I offer you my hand, you have saved my life."

Father then extended his hand, the witnesses joined in and a general reconciliation took place. *Tante* Aimée, short and stout, trotted on ahead, leading them to the big house where Grandmother was waiting and, as she reached the steps, *Tante* Aimée called to her mother, *"Chère Mère, regarde le beau spectacle que je t'amene,"* "Dear Mother, look at the beautiful spectacle I am bringing to you." Father sent for Mother who came out. And, with the drinks that were passed, more thanks and congratulations followed.

Aimée de Lobel

Poor Fannie was made to join the party and she looked as if she had surely borne the brunt of it all and we tried to whisper as our elders talked. It was certainly a case of much ado about nothing and most merry making for those who participated. I thank my stars that I live in another century and generation where duelling is unknown and no longer tolerated.

59

GROWING UP ON THE PLANTATION

Laura Plantation
as seen in the 1990s

Life, once more, began in earnest. Our studies and my piano kept me busy most of the day. We spent two months of the winter in the City, and rest of the year on the plantation. Father had always promised Mother that as soon as Grandmother divided the plantation and that he was in his own home, that she might have her late sister's children come and live with us.

Dédée Buard

The time had come and Louise, our "Mammy," Mother's old servant who had been living in Natchitoches, brought the children to us. Céline was six and Désirée, whom we called "Dédée," named for Mama, was four, These two became as one family and we lived as sisters and brother till they were grown, both calling me sister, as did George and Mimi, my own brother and sister.

Our only diversion on the plantation was horseback riding and we each had our own ponies. On one occasion that I remember, while riding with cousin Raymond de Lobel, who was on vacation from Fordham College in New York, my gray horse, "Magenta", suddenly ran away with me. Although I was a very good rider, I had not the strength to hold him in. I quickly realized that I would pass the country store owned by an old friend and that every man, black or white, would rush after me to stop my horse or that my horse might turn and go up the *levée*. I jerked my foot from the stirrup, closed my eyes and jumped.

I saw a thousand stars as my head struck the large ruts of the road. I was stunned but able to get up before Raymond reached me. As I had foreseen, my riderless horse passed the store, and a great excitement arose and my horse was caught and led back to me. I was jittery but insisted upon getting on again and I rode him to the front yard where he began to rear up with me. Then I knew I could not handle him anymore.

Raymond de Lobel

The news of my mishap had spread by the different negroes and George came heavy on his horse, frightened to death, thinking I was hurt. He got on "Magenta" with a whip. The horse reared and capered. George applied the whip and got him up the road, riding mercilessly for five or ten miles, whipping him all the time, till the poor beast, cowed and worn, was returned to his stable.

We later found out that the stableman, unbeknown to us, had run races on Sunday nights and won quite a bit of money on my horse, "Magenta". This, then, was the reason "Magenta" thought I wanted to race, when we rode together, my cousin Raymond and I.

There was a white fence around the big house to keep the animals out, but Mother had a second fence put up inside of that, closer to the house, where flowers and shrubs were planted. In those days, friends would visit and admire the garden, frequently asking for a cutting, which they could grow. And, there, outside the window of my bedroom, I planted a small begonia that had been given me. It lived for many years, growing to about three feet tall, blooming all over, every year, in its lovely pink bloom.

Planted there also were parmelee violets. They were very large and flat, about the size of a quarter. Louise, Mother's maid and a former slave, brought them from where she had visited relatives. These violets would let out the most fragrant perfume. They had to be thinned out every year and, soon, Mother had a very large bed of parmelee violets.

Once, while in New Orleans at Grandmother Locoul's house, Mother sent down a basket full of things from the plantation. She frequently did this when I was staying at Grandmother's on Toulouse Street behind the Opera House. This time, she put a large bunch of parmelee violets on top. I divided them with Fannie and Eugénie de Lobel. Each of us put a bunch on our coats and went out to the old St. Louis Cathedral. Soon, the perfume spread through the warm air of the church and heads turned to see from where the lovely fragrance was coming.

On Friday mornings, one of the local Acadians usually came on horseback to the plantation, peddling his waterfowl. They called the birds, *"poule d'eau,"* ducks that fed entirely on fish. It was the custom of the peddlers to arrive with the ducks slung on either side of their horses. When cooked and served with plenty of rice and vegetables, it tasted the same as chicken.

The Catholic priests even allowed *"poule d'eau"* to be eaten on Fridays, because they did not consider it to be a meat. The Acadians were the poor, uneducated whites. They seemed to have no ambition to learn, whereas you could always see the little negro children, every day, walking on the levee on their way to school, their blue "Appleton Spelling Book" up in front of the faces, spelling aloud: "B-A, B-A, K-E-R, K-E-R, B-A-K-E-R."

Riverboats
at New Orleans
1872

I was beginning to be restless for the companionship of friends of my own age and was up to every mischief to bring about a little decision. I would often stand on the front gallery facing the river, watching the big steamboats or packets pass by, imagining what fun and excitement it would be if an accident could happen to one of them (nothing serious, of course) in front of our place that we might go to the rescue of the passengers aboard and bring them home. Now, being an old and experienced housekeeper, I would worry to think where the food would come from to care for them.

But, in those days, such a minor detail was never thought of because the garden furnished enough vegetables of all kinds. The chicken house never had less than a hundred or more chickens and, at a pinch, a lamb could be killed. Three barrels of sugar and one of molasses was the supply kept for the year. Lard or cured hams and shoulders of bacon hung in the cellar, to say nothing of the large quantity of preserves and jellies made each summer which were enjoyed principally by guests, as we children were surfeited of them. And, I thought, if ever, when I was grown, and had a home of my own and saw fig preserves and cream cheese in a heart-shaped mold, with thick yellow cream, I would throw it out or run away. But, oh, how I would like to have it now.

Basement,
Laura Plantation

Dressing up in old clothes and playing the beggar woman had grown to be an old joke and I was suspected by the servants at once, so I had to work my fertile brain to think of some new and different pranks. Our attic had to be swept once a week, and windows opened to air it. On one occasion, a different old negro woman came to do the work and I saw my chance. Climbing the steep attic steps that led to a trap door, I went up and asked Ma Delcy if she wasn't afraid of ghosts. She replied that, indeed, she was not and continued sweeping vigorously, saying, "Go away, child, go away. I ain't got no time to fool with ghosts." Then, I said, "Well, if you don't believe me, come and see for yourself." And, tip-toeing softly and acting and gesticulating very mysteriously, I led her to a little old-fashioned sheep-skin trunk. It contained a plaster cast of Eliza, the family member whose portrait had been painted after death and this plaster cast made for it.

I lifted the lid, which squeaked for the hinges were so old. As I beckoned her to come, her curiosity got the best of her and, as she leaned over to look, I pulled a covering from the plaster cast and tore down the steps, intending to let down the trap door so that the old woman could not get out. But, I was too small and not strong enough and Delcy, close on my heels, mumbled to herself, "I done seen it, seen it with my own two eyes." And, rushing up to Mother, declared that no money could pay her to go up to that attic again for "that child had told the truth and she had seen a head just like a ghost." Mother's arguments and scolding were all in vain as Delcy marched herself to the quarters and she never changed her mind about the ghost in the attic of the big house.

It was around Halloween time and our yardboy, Jimmie, about sixteen, boasted of his bravery and that nothing in the world could ever scare him. So, another bright idea came to me to put Jimmie's boast to the test. It was his duty each evening to take over the overseer's supper in a large square basket which he carried on his head. I called George and, stealing sheets from our beds, we hid behind the wash house, a small building between our house and the overseer's. As Jimmie came with his basket on his head, whistling a lively tune, we rose from the ground, flapped our wings and groaned the most unearthly moans and groans and slowly groped nearer him.

Our terrific yell went up and down came the basket, supper and all, to the ground. Supper was ruined and crockery smashed and Jimmie had taken to his heels, screaming, "*Madame*, dere's ghosts behind the wash house and they would a caught me if I hadn't run." Mother was really furious this time because the supper was ruined and the china was broken to bits and she had to see about another supper being sent over, but, incidentally, not by Jimmie. We both caught a good scolding, although she always ended by laughing with us and seeing the funny side of it.

This same Jimmie was to have another sad experience while he was serving in the house. Father missed his pistol, an army revolver, a serious thing in those days, as every man, head of the house, slept with his pistol under his pillow. The servants looked high and low, but could not find it.

Suspicion pointed to Jimmie, as he had always expressed the desire for a pistol. So, Father sent for William, Jimmie's father, who was foreman on the place. Father told him of the incident, insisting that he was to say nothing to the boy, but keep a close watch on him to find if he had taken it.

But, William went back to the quarters, caught his son and beat him unmercifully. The boy swore that he never touched the pistol and remained in disgrace. Several weeks later, Father went to New Orleans, as was his habit each month to get money to pay the negroes. Upon entering his bedroom on 35 Bourbon Street, he saw his pistol behind the big bronze clock on the mantel, where he had left it the last time he had been to the City. Father was so distressed to think of the boy's unjust punishment that he was ready to make any amends, for he had the biggest heart in the world, that dear old dad of mine.

Bronze clock from Emile Locoul's Bourbon Street residence

Upon his return, Father immediately called Jimmie to his room and told him that he knew he did not take the pistol, as it had been found. And, handing Jimmie a crisp, new $5 bill, he asked if that would make up for the unjust beating his father had given him. Jimmie's eyes nearly popped out of his head with joy, exclaiming, "I'd take another beating if I could get five dollars for it again."

One of my mother's great challenges with negroes, especially the house servants, was to make them live respectable lives and to be married in the Church. The answer always came, "Lord, *Madame*, I ain't marrying that brute. If he beats me, I'm gonna hurt him."

Ranking foremost of these *protégées* of Mother's was Célestine, an old mulatto woman with a heart of gold, and the mentality of a child. She was the proud mother of a dozen or more children, ranging in color and nationality. Several of them could claim as their fathers the Sicilians who came up the river as beggars on pack boats to sell oysters, bananas, coconuts and apples. What a happy sound it was to our children's ears to hear, "Bananas, *Madame*, bananas," when they came around.

Célestine always filled in for any emergency when the cook or housemaid was sick or when any extra work was needed. As she grew older and was supposed to have been baptized a Catholic, Mother insisted that she marry Richard, her last husband, who was a good, faithful worker, so that she might go to Confession and Communion and follow her religion. Mother read the "riot act" to Richard and demanded that he take the little yard cart and mule and drive down Saturday evening to Church and be married by the priest. Richard mumbled, "I'd been married enough," but he submitted to Mother's dictum. She gave him money for the license and services and wrote a note to the priest with a history of Célestine's life, and they returned married. He remarried shortly thereafter. Several of Célestine's sons were trained as butlers but the daughters all went the way of their mother.

One of my many pastimes during vacation on the plantation was to tell fortunes with a Bible and key, reciting verses of "Solomon's Song" and watching if the key turned to say "yes" or "no." As Célestine was not a truthful person, I tried this on her with some amazing results. At the mention of the "Bible and key," she would fly away, saying, *"Bon Dieu Seigneur, la Bible va lui dire la vérité."* I had intended this for pure fun around the house as my good friend, Louise Braughn, had initiated me into how to work it.

One day, to my astonishment, the negro preacher from the back quarters came asking to see me. Hat in hand and with bowed head, he begged me to enlighten him upon some points about his church. I nearly passed away! I explained to him that I did this more so as a joke than anything, but, if he wanted to hold one side of the key and ask the questions to himself, then I would recite the verses and see what it says. His eyes grew wider and wider as he exclaimed under his breath, "Well, well." Evidently, the questions were answered to his satisfaction and he was a man thoroughly convinced. Then, he asked if he might return again when he was puzzled. I had the valid excuse that I would be soon leaving for the City and that ended the subject.

The negroes believed firmly, and with cause, in Voudoism, or the "Hoodoos." I never believed in it or understood it, but there was such a negro society in New Orleans. Anna, my old nurse, often told me about this society. One day, standing at the front door of our house on Bourbon Street, I saw Anna make a grand salutation to a big, masculine-looking negro woman who passed by. She told me later it was Marie Laveau, the "Queen of the Voodous."

To do harm or cause illness or the death of someone they disliked, they would sprinkle certain white powders mixed with chicken feathers, hair and some other absurd things on doorsteps. The person finding these signs at their door would be terrorized and get into trouble. It was said on the plantation, when one negro told another, "I'll put you where the dogs won't bark at you," he was sure to be found dead under mysterious circumstances.

The white people never paid any attention to these negro beliefs and were never harmed by them. Slavery was still too recent and the deep respect the negroes held for their former masters and their families in the big house was a wonder to see. To this day, I insist that I much prefer a good, southern negro to a common white servant. I grew up under their care and was always assured of their great devotion to us children. In case of any emergency, I would have called on them for protection.

I devoted much of my time to music and practiced several hours a day. The piano was going at different times of the day. Many evenings, all three of the de Lobel cousins met with us to play. Mother played the piano delightfully and we danced among ourselves, doing the square dance in those days.

I never had realized how musical and fond of music the negro race is. Another of Mother's young dusky *protégés*, working around the house, was called Bébé, who frequently could not be found to do his work because he had sneaked between the wall and the piano, lying flat on his stomach, listening to my practicing and, later, whistling all my tunes in the yard.

Writing of my music and my practicing reminds me of a funny incident about the old piano tuner who was a character. Once a year, he made the round of the Parishes, walking on the *levée* from plantation to plantation with a huge black umbrella which caused us to nickname him *"Monsieur Parapluie"* or "Mr. Umbrella." He usually managed to get to the house in the late afternoon, just before supper, spent the night, then worked the whole next day to tune my little pleyell. He spent the second night and left after breakfast on the third day, with his check of five dollars for the tuning. We figured that the fellow was brighter than he looked, making a fair living with free board.

Every traveler stopping overnight at the house, unless he were a tramp, was admitted to the table for meals and seated near the gentleman of the house. Many were the queer exhibit specimens that we had. They were the source of great amusement to us, especially the old mule man who came to sell mules. He was very chatty but had not the nicest smell about him.

Laura Locoul's copy of the "Bird Waltz" sheet music

Then, another man, a Dr. "Somebody," ate each time wearing a two-foot long, pointed, waxed goatee. He ended his hearty meal by putting his beard in his water glass and wringing it out straight again. This was too much and we children sneaked out the dining room, bursting with laughter. These were really the only excitements that we were allowed in those days of strict behavior. There was a large room at the back of the house for just such "guests" and they went to their rooms immediately after meals and were never a bother to the family.

It was the summer before I was thirteen years old that Lily LeGendre came to spend a few weeks on her family plantation, upriver from ours. She was beautiful to my childish eyes, and I worshiped her, and she was always that way to me.

One day she wrote me a note. She was possibly bored to extreme death, and the companionship of a child was better than none at all. It was a hot August day when I went to visit her and, after lunch, we put on thin wrappers and lay down on her bed to talk. My eyes grew bigger and bigger as she told me of her pleasures and conquests as a young lady and the wonderful time she had at Carnival. Then, she said, "Laura, you are just at the age when you ought to prevail upon your parents to send you to school in New Orleans so that you will grow up with the friends you should have when you come out. Governesses on the plantation will never get you anywhere."

Then, she told me of Mrs. H.G. Cenas' private boarding school which was the fashionable school of the day, where most of the nicest girls went, and that the school was only a short distance

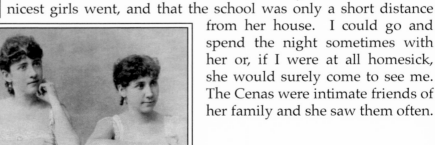

The two Sistene Angels (above) and the two Lauras Laura Maginnis (left) Laura Locoul (right)

from her house. I could go and spend the night sometimes with her or, if I were at all homesick, she would surely come to see me. The Cenas were intimate friends of her family and she saw them often.

When I returned home from Lily's that evening, I was no longer the child I had been. The turning point in my life had come and I was seeing things in a different light. I talked it all over with Mother that night and she agreed with me that it was just the thing for me, but Father had to be converted to the idea. There was the "rub," because parting with his children had never even entered Father's mind as yet, for, to him, home meant just wife, children and fireside.

I adopted the right tactics, I suppose, but I was not acting for I was restless and unhappy and longing with all my heart for what I wanted. For the next several weeks, I was the dullest individual on the plantation, and everybody could see the difference that had come over me. One day, in despair over my words, Father said anxiously, "Laurie, what is the matter with you? And, why are you so disconcerted?" I burst into tears, saying, "I am tired of the plantation, the negroes, mules and the horses. I want to go to school with girls my own age in New Orleans, see something, do something and be somebody."

I shall never forget the heart-broken look he gave me. "Where did you get these notions?" he asked. "Don't you love your father and mother and your family?" I said, "With all my heart, but that is not enough. I want to be as other modern American girls as I grow older and have friends." Well, Father went to Mother and she shared my feelings with him and, after many, many more talks and struggles than I can tell of here, it was decided that I should have my wish.

Pigeonier,
tool shed
& barn at the
Prud'Homme
plantation,
"Oakland"

BOARDING SCHOOL IN NEW ORLEANS

I entered Mrs. Cenas' School in February, 1876, and never was happier in my life. It was hard work and up-hill work, for I was not as advanced as the girls in my class. But, one's will and persistence can do much, and I kept up with them. I shall not say that I was not homesick, for the spells were terrible when they came. But, they soon passed and I count among the dearest friendships of my life those made right then and there. Dora Scott, who was in my class, has been my life-long friend. Many others who have since passed to the great beyond were in my class and those friendships were the truest and sweetest of my life.

Laura's
Report Card
dated 1877, age 15

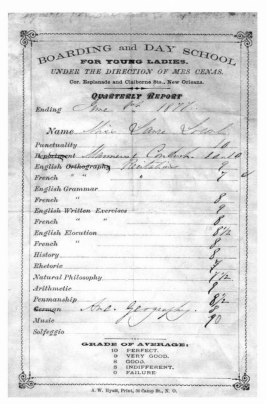

I had a splendid music teacher, *Mademoiselle* Romey, who was interested in me from the first. She said that I resembled one of her best pupils and hoped to make a duplicate of me. But, I fear, the dear lady was doomed to disappointment in me. Dear Mrs. Cenas taught both arithmetic and higher mathematics (I never reached that stage). Miss Heloise, who taught English, was wonderful and, in later years, she had a finishing school in Baltimore. Miss Clarisse taught French and was terribly strict, but I liked her best because that was just what always appealed to me.

Miss Anna had charge of the boarders and taught me to knit and crochet and to do fancy work. It was she who prepared us for our First Communion. Frances and Alice, the two youngest Cenas sisters, taught the little children upstairs. Alice married René Beauregard, son of the famous Confederate General, René Toutant Beauregard.

72

I made my First Communion on June 8th at St. Augustine Church and was confirmed two days later at the Jesuit's Church on Baronne Street. Mother came to be with me to see to my dress and things and to bring me my ivory prayer book and my tourmaline prayer beads that Grandmother Locoul gave to each one of her grandchildren when they made their First Communion.

I frequently spent Sundays at Grandmother Locoul's and my de Lobel cousins took me back in the evening. The years that I was in New Orleans brought Fannie de Lobel and me closer together than ever before, for we were nearly grown and very congenial.

Eugénie de Lobel was of an entirely different temperament. She was born old, brought up on the words *"convenances et comme il faut,"* that is to say, "do only what you should and what you must," which all of the rest of us rebelled against. She had a sweet disposition and never resented all our teasing.

Eugénie was very slow. It was a disease with her. She could never be ready to go anywhere and always got to church at the end of Mass. We, that is, Fannie and I, frequently missed our walks or wherever we were going because Eugénie could not be ready and, we always had to go with her. Grandmother and Tante Aimée de Lobel thought she was perfect and that we were the opposite!

The second year at school, Dr. Borde advised Mother not to let me board and live at the school as I had caught several children's diseases: measles, chicken pox, etc. The doctor said that a child so accustomed to open air and exercise as I should not be cooped up in boarding school.

Eugénie
de Lobel

So, I became a day scholar and lived at Grandmother's for the rest of the time. Grandmother, whose house was right behind the old Opera House on Toulouse Street, had a season box at the Opera. Her box was a *baignoire*, a prestigious seat where, every year, young debutantes would sit in order to watch and be watched.

French Opera House
on Toulouse Street
New Orleans

It was just the thing for me and Fannie de Lobel to go to the Opera twice a week. During the intermission between the acts, we would see the gentlemen leave the ladies to go to a little restaurant across the street. There, they would get what today we would call "hot dogs." But, back then we called them *"pattes toutes chaudes"* or little hot patties. The gentlemen would bring them back to the ladies in little white sacks. The ladies would take them, ever so delicately, in their white-gloved fingers and eat them. There were also small pastry shells with a top filled with oysters, chopped meat or chicken, oysters being the most popular. Men were never seen eating at the Opera, so they must have had theirs already, plus their drinks, while out getting the *pattes* for the ladies.

There was great distress that year from high water and Miss Romey gave a concert for the benefit of the homeless. The music was arranged for eight or ten pianos with two girls at each piano. Most of her old pupils, all young society girls, as well as a few new ones like myself, took part.

We were each to represent a flower and I was dressed as pink lilies of the valley. Each of the flowery ladies had to have an escort to accompany her on and off the stage and this was my stumbling block. I knew no boys! Finally, a cousin of Lily LeGendre whom I knew suggested her brother and, so, Seymour Gagnet was my escort. My partner at the piano was Minnie Koch, one of the belles of the City and I fell for her at once. She was so lovely and our friendship has lasted to this day.

The concert was a great success. I loved the rehearsals and enjoyed every minute of it and decidedly grew a foot taller in my own importance. Oh, how much I had to talk about when I returned to the plantation home during vacation. When everyone had gone to bed for the night, Mother and I would sit in the hammock on the end of the gallery of the big house, and she enjoyed all my silly chatter as if she were my own age. She really did relive her young life with me. After I was grown, I was thankful for every bit of sunshine I ever could throw into her life.

Front gallery
Laura Plantation

Poor, old Anna, my servant nurse from the plantation, came for me each morning to take me to school and called to pick me up at three in the afternoon. A group of us usually met at the corner of Canal & Rampart Streets and walked to school. Upon returning, we would buy coconut cakes and pralines from the old negro women who sold them at the street corners.

"Praline Seller"
a woodcut
by Lafcadio Hearn
1880

In New Orleans, the old negro women went around with baskets on their heads, calling out, *"Callas, toutes chaudes,"* "piping hot Callas," which were rice cakes shaped in a shell. They also carried *"vol-au-vents,"* those light, meat & sauce-filled pastries that some of us called "fly aways," or *"volaille,"* which was cooked chicken.

One time, when I had just left Grandmother Locoul's house on Toulouse Street (before we settled into our house on Bourbon), Mother made arrangements with one of the negro women vendors to bring breakfast every morning and dinner every evening. The grits, meat, fried potatoes and the rest were all brought in round tin pans, fitting one on top of the other, kept hot by a burner on the bottom.

My cousins, the de Lobels, went out very little socially because they were so very exclusive and only visited one or two of the old families. This made it hard for Fannie, who had more red blood in her veins and liked going out as any young girl of her age. As an outlet to a quiet life, she devoted most of her life to her piano and was a *pianiste* of note. Once, she was asked to play in a small, private musical at the home of an old family, the Montreuils.

I was also invited to attend and wore my Communion dress, with the addition of pink ribbon bows and was quite satisfied with myself. I had not been in the house but just a short time before I regretted having gone, on account of so many older people and I, the only school girl.

76

While I sat feeling quite out of place, I saw two tall, homely young men come in and speak to the host and one of them deliberately walked over to my side, smiled and said, "I believe that I need no further introduction to you, for I know that you are a little cousin of mine. I am Emile Archinard." Almost the same words his father, Alfred Archinard, many years before, had said to my own mother, when he saw her for the first time.

I was a bit nervous, but my short experience away from home had taught me that shyness and timidity were construed as dumbness. So, I plucked up my courage and did my best to appear at ease. Well, I must have succeeded in making some sort of impression for he never left my side, served me with refreshments and asked to escort me home. It was arranged for me to meet his family. His sister Alma was about my own age, and, right away, I fell for Mr. Archinard, Uncle Alfred, as we called him later, and the intimacy increased with the years.

In June, Father came to get me and, I suppose, I wanted him to see how I had grown up and, with much difficulty, persuaded him to spend the evening at the LaVillebeuvres, old friends of his, who had been lovely to me while I was at school in New Orleans. Father, over the last years, had dropped all his old friends, since he had lived on the plantation and had not seen many of them for years. His meeting with them did my heart good and, when I saw him bowing and scraping with his courtly old manners to Mrs. LaVillebeuvre, who always reminded me of an old dethroned queen, I nearly expired and could not get home soon enough to tell Mother about it.

The next morning, Father and I went to the Montreuils, another old friend of his, and where I had met Emile Archinard. Mr. Montreuil almost embraced him and they repaired to another room to talk over old times, with several decanters of wines beside them. We spent a most delightful evening and I felt I had done my father so much good.

On the following morning, we left for the plantation and, at seven o'clock, Emile Archinard was at the train to say goodbye to me. I was trembling in my boots, but Father was polite to him. When Father walked off to the other end of the platform, we talked. He asked me to write to him, etc. That was a blow to Daddy, to think that I was no longer a child, but he was still to be further taxed.

While Father sat reading his paper in the train, Alcée Fortier, a man easily double my age, entered the train and, after saluting Father, took his seat beside me. We chatted the whole two hours until we reached the Vacherie Station on our plantation. This same Alcée Fortier was the grandson of old Mr. Valcour Aime of St. James Parish, and he was later to become a very literary and distinguished man, having written one of the best <u>Histories of Louisiana</u>.

When we reached home and they were alone, Father poured out his grievances to Mother about the two young men whom he had seen provide me attention. She laughed and was terribly amused, much to his disgust.

Winter
on
Laura
Plantation

MEMORIES OF DEAR OLD DAD

Father was a most inveterate smoker and he always smoked cigars in New Orleans. And, while he was on the plantation, he could not be separated from his pipe. He smoked the real Perique tobacco grown in St. James Parish. Tobacco was tied up in carrots, one foot long, wrapped in sailcloth and bound with rope, which made it look corrugated on the outside when it was unwrapped. This was usually shaved into bits, dried before using and usually sold for five dollars a carrot.

Father had the carpenter on the place make him what looked like a crude little guillotine, a board with a circular hole cut to fit one end of the carrot and a sharp blade which was attached and used for shaving off the tobacco. On the mantelpiece of his room was a beautiful, huge cut-crystal jar with a top in which he held the shaved tobacco. It was my delight to run and fill his pipe for him.

Emile Locoul

Naturally, the troubles that Father had managing the plantation had made him sad and morose. The killing blow was when he had to borrow some money from a commission merchant to run the place and sign the first mortgage that had ever been placed on it. When he told Mother, he threw the papers into her lap, saying, *"Voilà, mon arrêt de mort."* "Here is my death warrant. I have never owed any man a dollar and cannot stand to be a borrower. I cannot live through it."

During that same summer, Father began to show signs of illness. I had never known him to be sick a day. The doctor diagnosed it as gastritis but he looked so well and was getting stouter. It was hard to realize that anything was wrong with him. Mother watched him closely, then, finally wrote to Dr. Borde, our family physician in New Orleans, telling him the symptoms she noticed.

Mother begged him to come up by an early morning train to see Father, promising to let him catch the evening train back to the City. He did so and, after a consultation with the country doctor, decided that it was Brights Disease that had turned into dropsy and that he should be operated on at once.

Everything was prepared for Dr. Borde to do it and, the relief was so great when the water was drawn from his side, that we were all wonderfully encouraged. Dr. Borde urged Mother to take him to New Orleans as soon as possible, but he dreaded the trip, and postponed it from week to week.

October had come and I should have been in school, but feared to leave Mother. Neither of us knew what to do. Finally, a second operation became necessary, and the country doctor made such a poor job of it that Mother concluded only Dr. Borde should touch him, should it become necessary again. So, it was decided that I should take Mimi with me to school and stay at Grandmother Locoul's until they came. George was sent to Jefferson College, across the River, and Céline to St. Michael's Convent, nearby.

On New Year's morning, Mother finally announced that he must let her take him to the City. She felt that another tapping would soon be necessary and there was no time to be lost. The servants prepared to close the house. Poor Father was dressed and made comfortable in a big armchair, which was carried to the *levée* to await the boat by four strong negroes. As soon as the news spread in the quarters, all the negroes came to the *levée* and, with bowed heads and tears streaming down their faces, bade him goodbye, some even kissing his hand as a last farewell.

Poor, dear soul, he took the ordeal manfully and, when he had been lifted by the same negroes and taken onto the boat, he turned with one long, lingering look at the place where he was born and which he knew he was leaving forever.

Later on that evening, a messenger came to tell me at Grandmother's that my family had arrived. I caught Mimi's hand and, without hat or coat, ran all the way to our house on Bourbon Street, until I was finally in his arms, looking, all the while, at Mother whose face showed the dreadful experience she had just passed through.

It was a joy, though, to have them in the City and near our beloved Dr. Borde, whom we all loved so dearly. With the wonderful care Mother gave him, he lived through the third operation and died on the 24th of March, 1879. As Mother called us in the middle of the night and I rushed to his side, putting my arm under his head, he gave me his last sweet smile of recognition and passed away; the water had gone up to his heart.

Weeks before, he had returned to his Faith and dear, old Father Jourdan of the Jesuits called to see him frequently. He was laid to rest in the Locoul tomb in the old St. Louis Cemetery on St. Louis Street. He rests between his father and mother but, unfortunately, owing to ill circumstances, the de Lobels (Tante Aimée and her husband) are laid in the upper compartments of the tomb, much to our sorrow.

We spent that spring and summer in New Orleans. George had been sent for during Father's last weeks of illness and had left Jefferson College to go to the Jesuits school afterwards. I left school and devoted my time to my music. My sister, Mimi, and Dédée went to day school at the Sacred Heart Convent and Mother began to re-adjust things as best she could.

Emile Locoul's
Death Notice

DÉCÉDÉ

Hier 24 Mars 1879,

Louis Raymond Emile Locoul,

âgé de 56 ans.

Les Amis et Connaissances des Familles LOCOUL, ARCHINARD et De LOBEL, sont respectueusement priés d'assister à ses funérailles, qui auront lieu CETTE APRÈS-MIDI à 4½ heures précises.

Le convoi partira de sa dernière résidence. Rue Bourbon No. 35, entre Douane et Bienville.

Nouvelle-Orléans, ce 25 Mars, 1879.

A vendre par J. BONNOT, 45 Rue Sainte-Anne.

SETTLING FATHER'S ESTATE

It was not long before preliminaries settling Father's estate began, taking an inventory and having me emancipated, that is, made of age by the law, so that I could sign for myself and relieve Mother of one less thing to be responsible for, as George and Mimi were still minors. Father left no will, but had given Mother the New Orleans house. The plantation belonged to us three children.

Mr. Legendre and his son, Jimmy, were our lawyers and advised us to sell some of the land back from the River to an Acadian, Mr. Joseph Webre, owning property in what was called *"La Vacherie."* We did so and almost wiped out the debt on the place. The sale of the Webre-Steib land paid off an old gambling debt of $16,000 incurred earlier by Father.

Jimmy LeGendre then made a proposition, to rent our place for three years and have his uncle, Mr. Agricole Armant, be overseer and superintend things. It seemed then a Godsend, for Mother was in poor health. My brother, George was too young and the arrangement seemed a good one as we still had the plantation home to go back to in the summer as usual. All worked out well for two years. There was a nice profit at the end of both years. After that, the prospects were not so good. The overseer had been looking mainly to the interest of Jimmy, his nephew, and was letting the place get into bad shape. Jimmy then asked to be released from the contract, which we were glad to do.

So, George, little more than a boy, began to be allowed to take charge. He loved the place with his whole heart and soul and it was the dream of his life come true. He had gone to the State University at Baton Rouge after Father's death and, before the end of the year, contracted typhoid fever there, which nearly cost him his life. It was months before he recovered at home.

George Locoul

In that summer of 1879, Uncle Alphonse Prud'Homme came to New Orleans where he always stayed at our house and, finding that I looked the worse for wear, took me back with him to Natchitoches where I spent the summer at Oakland. It was my first visit there since early childhood and I enjoyed it immensely. All the cousins my own age were adorable to me and gave me the time of my young life.

I was the "city girl" in town and the *belle* for the time being. Strange to say, the girls did not resent it but were my friends, also. When I left on the boat for home, I spent most of the night in my upper berth reading the parting letters that were sent me from my landing. I fell asleep wearing rings made from old gutta percha buttons and tiny baskets carved from the shell of large pecans and ever so many tokens sent me by my admirers.

Locoul sisters:
Laura (top) &
Noémie "Mimi"

The only cousin who showed me no attention while I was in Natchitoches was destined later to be one of my best friends and like a brother till the end of his life. This was Phanor Breazeale, who came to New Orleans to study law and he never forgot that our home was his while he struggled with a meager position to see him through his studies. I have no doubt that he would have lost heart and been discouraged but for the friends at 35 Bourbon Street who always helped and encouraged him. Breazeale was very successful in life and married Marie Chopin, whom I liked very much. Years later, Phanor Breazeale would be elected United States Senator from Louisiana. Both were my truest and best friends in all of Natchitoches.

OLD SWEET SPRINGS, VIRGINIA

In the early summer of 1880, Mrs. LeGendre asked Mother to let me accompany her to Old Sweet Springs, Virginia where they went every summer. Jimmy was going with her and her daughter, Lily (Mrs. Henry McCall). Her husband and children were to join her later on. It took a bit of planning before Mother decided to let me go. But, it was finally agreed that I could do so.

I had been dressed in deep mourning for over a year and was lightening the heavy, depressing black. I was then starting to wear white and gray and having my first real evening dress, for Virginia was synonymous with dancing.

Old Sweet Springs,
Virginia

Minnie Koch, then one of the *belles* of New Orleans and a bride-to-be in winter, was there with her brother, Herman. They both were intimate friends of the LeGendres and we were one, big, happy family. Jimmy and Herman almost ran the place; they were such popular *beaux*. I was able to share a little bit of their popularity by being the youngster of the party.

Doctor Chester Mayer of New York was at one table and was very anxious to be one of our party and did a very nice thing for me, indeed. It was announced that a large crowd of the older *belles* and *beaux* of New Orleans, summering at White Sulphur Springs, were coming over for the day at the Old Sweet. Immediately, it was decided that a moving *German* would be gotten up in their honor and Dr. Mayer was going to lead it.

That evening, he asked me if I would lead it with him. I accepted, not knowing what I was saying! And, frightened out of my wits, ran to Lily McCall's room and told her what had happened and asked her what I should do and how a *German* was danced, for I had never seen one in my life. She laughed at my panic and told me all I had to do was to follow my partner and lead as he told me to and not to be frightened.

The thought of blundering or being awkward or doing something absurd before that crowd of New Orleans people whom I would meet the following winter, put me through torture. Well, the day arrived and, dressed in my best white dress and leghorn hat, I met Dr. Mayer in the parlor and we proceeded to the dance hall.

When I entered the hall and saw all those familiar faces, all fear deserted me at once and, starting off with my partner, led the most intricate figures, with never a hitch, as if I had danced it all my life. My assurance came from the comforting way in which my partner whispered to me what to do. It was very simple entertainment to those old veterans who had been dancing *Germans* winters in and summers out. To me, though, it was a never to be forgotten day of triumph and enjoyment!

In speaking with New Orleans men from the White, I found out accidentally that one of the most popular girls there that summer was Lily Buckner of Louisville. I wrote her a note that I was to be in New York in a few weeks and that I hoped to meet her there. She had been to boarding school with me and I loved her dearly.

From the Old Sweet, we went to the White for a week. Mrs. LeGendre wanted to take a few sulphur baths for her rheumatism and I was broken-hearted to leave the crowd of good friends I had made at the Old Sweet and we had a great oration of farewells at the train station.

At the White, by the time we arrived, the season was dead and only a few stragglers remained. However, in a few days, I was introduced by a man I had met that summer, to a homely, old fellow named Bruce Morgan. He was on the staff of "Andrew's American Queen," a New York magazine, and he deluged me with poetry.

I found verses near my plate at the table, received them in the mail and even used Mrs. LeGendre as a shield to avoid talking with him or going with him anywhere. I was written up every week in his magazine as "the attractive little dark-eyed creole from New Orleans" until I thought I would go mad trying to dodge him. At last, Jimmy LeGendre came one night and we left the next morning for New York. For at least four or five years, I received letters and poetry from him.

NEW YORK

New York! Well, it is just the same feeling that every girl has upon seeing the big city for the first time. We stopped at the New York Hotel where all southerners stopped. It was like being home again. Many of my old schoolmates were there and our party met again and it was one grand, jolly, happy trip! I had my photograph taken at Faronis for Mother and bought my winter outfit and we left for the old home that we were always glad to get back to.

But, another excitement was still in store for us. Upon our return near Montgomery, Alabama, at 3 o'clock in the morning, our train went down an embankment. Pandemonium reigned. The men thought we had plunged into the river because a water cooler had upset in one of the berths. Jimmy was the first to break a window and he managed to crawl out of the train, reassuring us that we were on "terra firma." Then, Mrs. LeGendre began to jabber in French, saying such utterly ridiculous things that I was almost in hysterics.

I had laughed all summer long and, feeling ne'er a bruise nor a broken bone, it was only natural for the humorous aside to appeal to me since none of us were hurt. When a man called out, "For God's sake, give me something that looks like a pair of pants," that was my undoing!

My only concern now was getting my small satchel in which I had Mother's diamonds. When she had loaned them to me for the summer, she said, "I never expect to see them back." It was a question of honor with me that she should get them back as I had been very careful with them. And, she did get them back since my satchel was one of the first to be tossed out of the wrecked train car. So, then, I immediately made myself presentable in the dark.

Laura Locoul
in her
New York
photograph

At daylight, we were taken in by some farmers who gave us pails of hot water, soap and towels to take the grime from our faces. More hysterics followed because Jimmy LeGendre looked like a big, black devil. He was so dirty and I was not much better looking myself. Mrs. LeGendre was truly irritated by our hilarity. The whole event had been anything but a joke to her as she thought that her little grandson had been killed in her arms. But, every time that Jimmie and I looked at each other, we burst out again!

In the meantime, my poor mother at home was frantic when we failed to reach New Orleans on time. And, even though it was reported that a baggage train had been derailed and held up the passenger train, her fears were not to be quieted. She sent word to dear Dr. Borde to be on-hand if needed, with every preparation made for the worst. Our carriage finally arrived at the front door of our house and I jumped out and into her arms, laughing again and happy to be home.

It seems that, just at three o'clock on the morning of the wreck, Mother was suddenly awakened by my voice calling her. Mother said that she ran to the door to unbolt it and got even down to the front door to find no one, of course. But, this uncanny call of mine only added to her fears, and she felt sure that some trouble had befallen us until we arrived. Oh, how much we had to talk about for the longest time afterwards.

Upon my return, I was told that Andrew Friedrichs was engaged to Jeannie Michell. We were invited to his house to meet his friends and Jeannie asked me to be one of her bridesmaids. I was willing as it was the first time I had ever been in a wedding party. I stood with Dr. Fred Parham. I found Bussiere Rouen engaged, also. It seems, because I went away with the LeGendres, that I was considered engaged and it was quite amazing, until, finally, the impression was changed and my friends would believe me, that I was heart whole and fancy free.

A REMNANT OF FORMER GRANDEUR

O f all the many places of interest that a stranger would delight in visiting while rambling through the sunny South, is one that recurs to me constantly as the dearest, loveliest and most romantic spot in Louisiana.

Situated on the Mississippi River, a mile above Grandmother Locoul's plantation, is an extensive sugar plantation belonging years ago, in the palmy days of Louisiana, to owners whose wealth was boundless and whose noble descent entitled them to the position they held as first in the land. Being of a proud and lofty nature, the Aime family enjoyed life in the most luxurious manner, among themselves alone; excluding strangers and even marrying and intermarrying for several generations.

Back gallery
Valcour Aime's
"Petit Versailles"
1880s

Monsieur Valcour Aime, master of these vast possessions, was a kind and generous man, but proud and ambitious as well, and his chief desire was to embellish the old homestead which already ranked as one of the handsomest plantation homes in the state. The house had large spacious rooms adorned with paper on the walls of the most fantastic designs and some even representing historical subjects, wide galleries extending around and wide, brick steps leading to a court below. On special occasions, the slaves were given a holiday and were permitted to feast in the court and to enjoy themselves in their many rustic ways, while their masters viewed the merry scene from the gallery above.

One thing remained to complete the grandeur of this beautiful home in the eyes of the proud, old master, and this was a garden (such as he had seen abroad) that would surpass anything here in America. Just at that time, my father had been sent to France to be educated. Father had just distinguished himself at the Royal Military Academy at Bordeaux and was travelling through Europe before returning to Louisiana. It occurred to Mr. Aime that a French gardener, by trade, could best carry out his great idea and he consequently applied to my young father to secure for him, regardless of cost, the finest gardener that could be obtained from the *"Jardin des Plantes"* in Paris. The desired personage was secured with very little difficulty and was sent to America.

The gardener was known as *"Monsieur* Joseph" and, at once, began to prepare the beautiful grounds entrusted to his care. Soon, he gave startling proofs of his being an artist as well as a very fine gardener. A number of slaves were placed under his command to execute the work and the finest trees and palms were imported from abroad. The walks were lined with shrubbery and pretty evergreens while the most intricate designs were traced and laid out with the choicest plants. Shady nooks and arbors, covered with honeysuckle and ivy, stood invitingly at every turn.

Beautiful hothouses filled with imported plants bearing blossoms of every kind occupied the four corners of the grounds. Iron pipes were inserted into the ground so as to keep the required temperature of heat in winter. Springing in the center of the garden and circling through with undulating grace was a small, artificial river shaded on either side by many a majestic old oak, whose wide and spreading boughs drooped as low as the water's edge. Tall magnolias, covered with snowy blossoms, gladdened the sight and the faint sweet olive filled the atmosphere with its delicate perfume.

Had Longfellow known of the picturesque beauty of this little stream, he might have induced the "fair maid of Acadia" to wend her weary steps towards these shady banks and linger there a while, before resuming her search for her much loved Gabriel.

Aime Family in front of the Petit Versailles manor

Following the course of this river to the left of the garden, a wide stone bridge was reached. It led to a miniature island so pretty and attractive to the eye, as to cause one to stop and wonder how the banished hero of France could have found aught but sheer contentment and peace in his exiled home if it bore resemblance to this lovely spot named in memory of Napoleon's last home, the "Island of St. Helena."

Upon this island was built a small fort, with port holes cut into the rock and a cannon of diminutive size, which was taken away by the enemy during the War. A bronze mastiff stood at the entrance of the island as if to protect the fort. Just below, leading to the water's edge, was a step cut into the stone for the purpose of descending into small boats kept around the island for the ladies to paddle around in the long, summer evenings.

As the island receded in the distance, one could imagine himself removed to a mountainous country because high and steep before him rose a mountain of considerable size by the work of man. A winding path hedged with bright wildflowers brought anxious visitors to a cool and lovely pavilion at the very top, cozily furnished with iron chairs and tables. Beneath this hill was a grotto, said to have been built there by Valcour Aime during the last years of his life when he spent his days in prayer and penance after the death of his favorite child, Gabriel.

Taking a view of the right of the garden, could be seen, peeping from a mass of ivy, a small billiard room fitted up in the most exquisite taste. Nearby, a fountain could be seen beneath a ruined wall and it was covered with the same species of creeping vine. A romantic supposition was that couples, if they were sentimentally inclined, might exchange an ivy leaf with the emblem and make a wish and the wish was sure to come true in the end. Two huge camphor trees stand on either side of the house, said to have been imported from China as mere shoots and were, probably, the only ones in Louisiana.

This masterpiece of labor and toil flourished for many years in all its splendor until the trouble between the north and south took place, and among the most unfortunate victims of the War were the Valcour Aimes. Endowed by nature as well as with worldly goods, this prosperous family knew nothing of the trials and the miseries of the outside world and, when the knowledge of their ruin came upon them, it came like a crash. The wheel of fortune had turned and they found themselves bereft of every acre that had been their own for nearly three-quarters of a century and they were thrown upon the cold world.

Oh, if one has not felt the anguish of bidding a last farewell to the old family homestead, then one can little conceive the pain and despairing feeling that creeps over one's spirits and clings there for so many a weary day.

Well, the place passed into the hands of strangers, who entrusted it to the care of overseers. These practical men, with little or no poetry in their soul, considered that sugarcane paid, while flowers did not, so the fields were made to flourish and the garden was left to destruction.

Petit Versailles house in ruins

Oh, how well I remember it still, the dear, old place, where I spent so many blissful hours, and had so many queer experiences, where I listened with a beating heart to the low, sweet pleadings caused by all the inspiring sur-roundings, and especially in the Springtime, when "a young man's fancy lightly turns to thoughts of love."

But, Alas!, it is all gone now. Its beauty has vanished like some fair dream, leaving what can now be seen, a wreck of former days. The paths are overrun with weeds and the hothouses are nearly destroyed. The billiard room, pavilions and arbors have been blown away by storms. The river is low and marshy and the bridge has been carried away. Only the "Island of St. Helena" and the mountain remain to interest the stranger who visits it now.

Guests are always welcomed within its gates, and, upon entering the great, big iron gate, where many of the bars are bent by lightening, Pa André meets you. He is an old slave of the place, allowed by the new owners, to live in his same old cabin. His greeting is so respectful and manners so courtly, as to assure you that his master was a true, old *"gentilhomme"* of the old school.

Bent and infirm, old Pa André moves with the air of becoming dignity, accompanying his guests through the garden, taking the greatest pride in relating family history, telling of the sumptuous feasts and gorgeous weddings and, when, on occasion, the garden was lit up with Japanese lanterns and supper was served in the center of this enclosure that resembled a fairy scene. He ends each description with a deep sigh and then exclaimed, "Ah, but now, it ain't like it was before the War, when old *Monsieur* was here."

Returning to the house, *Tante* Célina meets you. She is the old man's wife, and a quaint dried-up looking, little woman she is, wearing the proverbial blue cottonade dress tucked up at the waist, with a white kerchief 'round her neck and a colored *tignon* on her head. Holding her dress in one hand, she bows, making a low curtsy as she welcomes you and disappears.

Soon, she returns with an earthen pitcher with fresh and sparkling water from the cistern and bright colored glasses in a red wooden tray and offers to her guests the most cooling beverage she has. As you depart, they accompany you as far as the gate on the main road, bidding you, *"Adieu"* and "Come again soon," with all the grace of manner becoming many a great lady and gentleman.

MY DEBUT

In the winter of 1882, I made my debut in a beautiful dress that Mrs. Denègre gave her daughter, Lily, my friend and schoolmate. I wore a white satin that was really most attractive, made by *Madame* Marchand, a very fine French dressmaker. Clusters of white roses held the shoulders, and one white bud was tucked into my hair.

Laura Locoul
in her
white evening gown,
1882

Jimmy LeGendre escorted me to the ball and, in real big brother fashion, took me and brought me back, with no further thought of me. Fortunately, the men asked to be introduced and, in no time, my programme for the evening was filled. I was given a partner for supper, and my only concern was trying to remember the men I had never met before and whose names were on my programme.

It all seemed like a beautiful dream and, when I returned home at four in the morning, the satin on one slipper was nearly almost black from the hands of the men (although they wore gloves). This elicited the amusing remark from my old nurse, Anna. She said, "I didn't know white gentlemen had such dirty hands."

Laura as "Mephistopheles" at the *Semmes Debut Fancy Dress Ball, 1886*

Anna was called in to see me dressed before I went to a party, and I heard the same exclamation each time from her, "Now, that is the beautifullest of the beautiful," as I stood in front of the *armoire-à-glace* for her inspection. Anna then departed to her room to get some sleep before I returned, for I carried no latchkey. It would have been of little use, for Mother had two prison bolts, as I called them, on the door that were always locked at night. I never waited more than just the few moments it took the poor, old soul, Anna, to get downstairs to open the door for me.

When I reached my own room, I very frequently found Kit, a young negro girl we had for several years, sleeping on the floor before the fireplace to keep the fire burning when I arrived. Kit would help me out of my dress. She was not expected to do this, but did it of her own accord because she was devoted to me. Being just about my size, Kit inherited many of my discarded dresses. That made her the *belle* of the worker's quarters when she went back to the plantation in summer.

The rest of the winter was a round of countless balls, dinners and luncheons until Carnival came and ended it all for a while. No matter how worn out I was and was the last to leave the French Opera House on Mardi Gras night or the next morning, I always went to church on Ash Wednesday to receive the ashes and begin Lent well, if possible.

GRANDMOTHER LOCOUL'S DEATH

In October of 1882, Grandmother Elisabeth Locoul died at the age of 84, and was buried in the family vault at the St. Louis Cathedral Cemetery. A most unfortunate mistake was made when they opened the compartment where my father was placed. Mother was called to the cemetery and Father's remains were dropped to the bottom of the tomb to where his father's remains were. For us it was a horrible tragedy and a terrible experience for my own, dear mother to undergo so shortly after Father's death.

More trouble and dissensions erupted again when Grandmother Locoul's succession was settled. Accompanied by our lawyer, Jimmy LeGendre, George and I went to Grandmother's house to have the inventory taken of her estate and personal possessions. And, though things should have been equally divided, we came out at the short end and a renewed coldness ensued between the two families.

Tante Aimée claimed the best of the furniture. The real estate that we inherited from the old property in the old French Quarter was depreciated so much that our share amounted, when sold, to eighteen thousand dollars, to be divided among us three. Had it been invested, we might still have had a nest egg, but, it was all swallowed up in the plantation in the next few years.

Manor House
Laura Plantation
1990

FROM MOURNING TO MARDI GRAS

We, of course, had to wear black. At the time, I had just had enough of a taste of society to chafe at the thought of mourning, especially when it was not in my heart. However, during October and November, I was very good. But, toward the latter part of December, invitations came out for a very large fancy dress party given by the T.L. James' family on Prytania Street.

Mother said that, of course, I could not go, for she would be blamed by the relatives and I would be severely criticized. Well, I stood it until I thought I would burst! A week before the ball, I went to my desk and sent in my acceptance letter. But, that was not all. I had to get a costume!

My brain started to work quickly and I remembered a fancy dress that a friend of Mimi's, my sister, had described to me as being simple and attractive: the costume of a baker girl. In counting up my small change and relieving George and Mimi of theirs, I went to the D.H. Holmes store and purchased several yards of their white Turkish toweling.

Then, I went to see *Mme.* Rosa Reynoir, a milliner who had made our hats since we were little children. I told her my plight and asked her to make me a tam-o-shanter cap and to be <u>mum</u> about it. *Madame* Reynoir was greatly amused, said she was interested and insisted that it would be her contribution to my costume, provided that I came and told her all about it and how it all ended.

Then, I stopped at Victor Bero's Restaurant, a very exclusive French restaurateur whom Father had helped in his earlier days and whose food was adored by all of us. I told him my little secret and asked him to make me a dozen very small breads for the breadbasket that I was to carry on my arm.

Laura Locoul
in her black bustle

He entered into the spirit at once and was highly interested, sending me the most adorable little french bread loaves, *avec ses compliments*, and refused any mention of pay.

In the meantime, I had been working like a bee in the top story of Grandmother Locoul's house and had finished my shirt. Mother walked in on me at the house, she seemed greatly surprised and reiterated all of her same objections, which was surely on account of the relatives. In the end, though, I won out.

And then, the dear, sweet soul that she was, Mother turned around, giving me the biggest assistance in making me a darling little apron, getting fancy slippers for me and loving it just as she always had.

When I reached the James' that night, the boys made a dash for the loaves. We threw bread at each other; the hilarity was endless, and it was glorious. At 12 midnight, the huge tree was lighted and Santa came down to distribute the presents. Supper was served and we danced until four in the morning.

As we were leaving, Mrs. James, the hostess, put her arm around me and said, "Laura, your costume was so attractive and different from all the shepherdesses, Marguerites, Spanish ladies, etc." "But," I said, "Mrs. James, I was the only common peasant in the room." She stooped and, kissing me, whispered, "And the most original and fascinating." In my own mind it had been such little trouble and I went home very well pleased with myself and the wonderful time I had had.

The next morning, bright and early, I wrote appealing, little notes to the society reporters of the "Picayune" and "Times," begging them please to keep my name off the list of the James' party for very personal reasons.

New Year's 1884 came next. Several girls usually congregated at one house and received, in full evening dress, by gaslight. Mémée Folwell asked me to receive guests at her place, for I could not receive at my own house under the circumstances. And, I had to compromise with Mamma on a white evening dress. We all had a glorious day. There were as many callers as at many of the other parties, and there was great rivalry as to who would have the most men calling. Every card gathered in the card file was religiously counted. After that, it was easy sailing, and I was in full swing with the winter.

Invitation to the 1884 Rex Ball

Rex Ball favor,
a silver pill box,
engraved:
"Rex Feb. 22, 1887
Laura Locoul"

Annie Howard was Queen of the Carnival that year and she asked me to be one of her Maids of Honor in the Court of Rex. It was a grand winding up to a glorious winter. My duke was Tom Sloo, one of the most handsome men in New Orleans, and I was the Duchess of Bourbon. When my duke called for me in one of the open Royal carriages, he was all bedecked with the colors of Rex, and each of the livery coachmen and footmen was wearing his own scarf across his chest.

I was carrying an enormous bouquet provided by the King. We crossed Canal Street and the crowd gave us right of way as we proceeded to the Boston Club to witness the procession. I almost thought it was true, and that I belonged to the Royal Family.

After the Rex ball, at midnight, we rushed to the French Opera House to the ball of Comus, where the two Courts would always meet and exchange Queens for the Procession. Afterwards, we repaired to the Howard's mansion where a sumptuous supper was prepared.

And, then, we were all ready for sackcloth and ashes. And, be it said again, that, no matter how tired I was or at what time of the morning I left the doors of the Opera House, I never failed to get to Mass and receive the ashes of Ash Wednesday and try to make a good beginning for Lent.

Laura (right) with her friend, Julia Braughn, 1887 Queen of Carnival *at the* *Laura Plantation*

BEST FRIENDS

The next month, Mother was taken quite sick and was in bed for many weeks with kidney trouble. The doctor said she must have a change and absolute rest.

Back gallery
Laura Plantation,
1887
Top left, going clockwise:
house maid, Désirée,
Julia Braughn, George,
Susie (Mimi's friend),
Mimi and Laura
playing her banjo

The family at Bourbon Street was quite large, counting the two cousins, Céline and Dédée Buard, that Mother had taken in after her only sister's death. Their father, Alex Buard, had never done a thing for them, and Mother said she had thought seriously and frequently during her illness of what a care she would leave to me if anything had happened to her.

Mother said that Uncle Alex must understand his obligation to his children. She wrote him that it was time for him to assume the responsibility, as she had cared for his daughters during their most trying age and that she was no longer strong enough to do it. Uncle Alex came for them and Mother fitted them with everything to make their little home comfortable. Friends sent them presents and, like children, they were delighted at the prospect of the trip back home. Later, I fear, they had cause to bitterly regret leaving, but, both married at an early age and had large families.

Then, we began to plan our own trip. I suppose that I did most of the planning, as Mother and I were congenial. During the time that we would be away, Mother was having the house in New Orleans painted, an arch put between the two parlors and the whole place generally repaired, as it was badly needed.

We went to old Point Comfort for July, and loved it there. The sea bathing was lovely and I met a number of people. Dora Scott, my dearest chum, had written to several of the young lieutenants at Hampton Roads, whom she had known as Cadets at West Point. Dora asked them to call on me and give me a good time, which they certainly did. One of my good friends at the resort, Lannie Gooth, was there with her mother and we became very friendly. Mrs. Gooth and Mother were quite congenial. George and Mimi had their young friends and enjoyed the place in their own way.

Then came the great moment! We left for the Greenbrier at White Sulphur Springs. Laura Maginnis, her mother and brother, Albert, were already at the White and many others from New Orleans were there, also. The morning after our arrival, Branch Miller, a young lawyer, and one of the favorite *beaux* in New Orleans, asked me to dance the *German* with him, which was a lovely thing to do for a newcomer. He introduced me to all the young men there at the time. It was all I needed! From that time on, it seemed so beautiful to be there.

Sue Richardson, Annie Miller, May Bickham and others came with their families. Many New Orleans men spent their vacation there. For the next three weeks, it was nip and tuck between Richmond and New Orleans, but our men were so true and loyal to us that I think New Orleans kept the lead in attendance.

White Sulphur Springs,
West Virginia

A bunch of West Pointers, just graduated, spent their vacation at the White and, while dancing the *German* one night, my partner, a handsome six-footer, Clarence Edwards, snapped his fingers, saying, "Golly, but you remind me of a friend of mine." After hearing this remark two or three times, I asked the name of his friend at West Point.

Clarence said, "You don't know him, his name is Powhatan Clark." I said, "You don't mean Powie Clark?" Then he straightened up and said, "Yes." "Why, he is a cousin of mine," I said. The man seemed so unbelieving that I caught his arm and took him to the end of the big banquet table where Mother was seated with other chaperones and asked her to verify my statement. She did, of course, and we raced back to our places.

Then, Clarence called Henry Cabel, of Virginia, and Jim Shipp, all classmates of Powie's, and they were adorable to me; Shipp especially, as he was Powie's closest friend. Jim Shipp was killed during the Cuban War, years later, going up San Juan Hill. Clarence was killed during the World War in 1914 and Cabel I lost touch of.

We remained at the White six weeks after the season was over and, I must admit, I felt and looked like a dish rag and was sure that, if any man asked me to dance again, I would brain him on sight.

Laura Maginnis and I had become very close friends and we decided to leave both our families together to head for New York. We would take rooms together at the old New York Hotel, where we stayed nearly a month. We had a grand time there, also, as some of the men we had met came to New York, and some of the home men were passing through and they took us to the theatre. Laura Maginnis and I both visited Clara Dobson, of New Orleans, now Mrs. William Danning in West Orange, and enjoyed seeing that entire part of the country.

It was getting time for home, but I could not be outdone by Laura Maginnis, not at this stage of the game. She was going to visit in Louisville and I had been invited by Natalie Clarkson Greene to visit her in St. Louis. According to the strict ideas of the day, it was not in keeping with the rules of propriety that I should travel alone from New York to St. Louis, for the big bad wolf might be hungry on the way and might have caught me.

These things were not done on the spur of the moment and, after much arguing and planning, Mother decided to change her tickets at a great loss and go home by way of St. Louis.

Natalie Greene was staying in Webster Groves, just outside of St. Louis. Her family was charming to me as were Mr. & Mrs. Claiborne, her parents, and her sister, Mrs. Robert McCormack Adams. Natalie had an unmarried cousin, Henry Edmonds, later Judge Edmonds, and he took us to the Veiled Prophet ball in the old Merchant's Exchange and we spent the night in St. Louis with another cousin of Natalie's, Mrs. Boyle.

Among the men that Henry introduced me to was Winston Garrett and he gave me a rush during the visit, and it lasted for a year or two. He was tall, handsome, belonged to one of the best families there, and had a buggy and horse and drove me to Webster Groves several times when I was in town.

Laura Maginnis then visited Mrs. D.R. Powell with her mother. Mrs. Powell included me in a large tea which she gave Laura. I wore a royal blue velvet outfit that Mother had given me in New York. Winston sent me a gorgeous corsage of Marshall Hill roses and drove me back to Webster the next day.

One evening I drove out with Mrs. Adams in Webster and she stopped to see a friend. Not having told me the friend's name, I did not know at whose house I was going. After our cards were sent up, a tall blonde girl walked up and, who should it be, but Jeannie Lockwood! We both gasped and then opened our hands and rushed for each other. I had met her earlier in the summer at old Point Comfort. From that day began a friendship which was the turning point of my life and one that has lasted through the last fifty or sixty years.

She was lovely to me, inviting me several times to her house. She visited me in New Orleans at Carnival a year or so later, and I was one of her bridesmaids when she married Walker Hill, of Richmond, Virginia. At this wedding I stood with Charles Henry Gore, the man who became my groom in April, 1892, when he transplanted me from my native soil to St. Louis.

Jeannie lived for several years in Richmond and, upon her return to St. Louis to live, insisted upon my visiting her in her cute little home on West Pine. It was a lovely visit, indeed. The Hills did all they could for my pleasure and gave me a beautiful time.

MY BEAU

While I went out with all the *beaux* of St. Louis, especially that select group known as the "Bull's Eye Club" of the old St. Louis Club, Charlie Gore stood in the background, never interfering, never trying to cut ahead of the others, always so retiring. But, I knew, by that indefinable something that always whispers to one, where Charlie's feelings were for me, and it was just before the eve of my departure for home that he told me of his love and asked me to be his wife.

There are reams and reams that I could write about, for we were both sentimental and sensitive natures, but, I have always considered courtship and marriage so sacred that to air it in public, even for one's own children alone, robs it of its sanctity. The humorous part is, of course, that our engagement was to be a deep secret, and none suspected it, even until six years later when we finally announced it.

So, when I left the next evening, Charlie had told me that he would ride with me as far as Carbondale, Illinois, several hours from St. Louis. At the train station, old Will Provenchere told me he was going to ride across the bridge with me. He also had a little secret to impart. But, when I told him that Charlie Gore had asked permission to ride that far with me, he snatched his ticket from his pocket and tore it up.

Charles H. Gore

A few moments later, Jim Lockwood, Jeannie's brother, who had made our last evening at Jeannie's pretty miserable by sticking around, declared he was going to see me last. Going over the bridge with me, I had to tell him that Charlie had asked me first. And, his ticket was, likewise, torn into bits, with a few epithets to the luckiest man.

Charles Gore with Laura Locoul in his surrey, St. Louis, 1886

Charlie adored music and, I think my playing just attracted him to me, for he always begged me to play for him whenever a piano was in sight. But, Jim Lockwood <u>detested</u> music and, when he pestered us, my last evening in St. Louis, the only way I could send him upstairs to Jeannie's room was by playing the grand quartet from *"Lucia de Lammermoor,"* with both pedals pushed to the floor and making as much noise as I could manage from the piano.

ADIEU, LOUISIANA

I returned home to Louisiana very happy, but found much to worry me as things were not prospering on the plantation. A mortgage had to be placed on the farm and, even with my short experience, I knew it was the beginning of the end! Four generations had been born and reared there. It had always been called "the chicken that laid the golden egg," for the ground was very fertile and productive. The place, at a higher elevation than most of the surrounding country, had never once suffered from the dreadful crevasses that inundated so many of the beautiful plantations around.

But, all good times come to an end. We were forever in the hands of commissioner merchants who were, more or less, shylocks, and we struggled for another two years. George did his best, poor boy, but the odds were against him. The price of sugar was so low that it did not pay for the production and for wages to the negroes. But, we held on, making the best of it until the day of reckoning should arrive.

Duparc & Locoul sugarmill, 1888
From far left: Ivan de Lobel, George Locoul and laborers

The last Christmas on the old plantation was so memorable that, to my dying day, it will be vividly impressed upon me. We always had lots of company with the boys coming up Saturday afternoon until Monday morning. Charlie made two visits that spring and fall, and I always managed to keep the others away at that time, so that none ever suspected my engagement, not even Mother. My love came to me and spent four blessed days with me at "the Laura." The days were perfect and the birds never more sweetly sung and "our spirits rushed together at the touching of the lips."

Charles H. Gore

Will Provenchere, of St. Louis had been invited for Christmas to see us, in the most casual way, just as dozens of others always were invited for the holidays. We always said, "Come on down sometimes, anytime," never expecting people to show up. But, two days before Christmas, Will came down, a perfect stranger to my family.

Jim Theard, of New Orleans, dear, old Jim, the best friend a girl ever had, usually came to visit us at this time and he came loaded with boxes of candy and special gifts for me and for Mimi, also. At the sight of a lovely hat that Jim brought me in a long velvet case, with a delightful box of candy buried inside, Provenchere turned white and concluded that I was engaged to Jim.

On Christmas Eve, Will McGary blew in. Will was quite the bragadoccio kind whose heart would never be broken by any girl. When he saw me with three men on my hands to entertain, he whispered to me, "I'll leave tonight, but, may I return next week and hear the results?" Well, was I ever thankful for one less.

Jim Theard was, more or less, at home on the place and went off with George. But, come Christmas morning, alone in the old main parlor with a big, roaring log fire, Prov proceeded to unburden his heart and tell me the reason of his visit. Old Prov was a tall, fine looking man, but <u>very emotional</u>, true, honest and sincere. It was a chaotic morning I never want to duplicate again.

Finally, Jim and George returned to the house and dinner was announced. Mother had a lovely dinner prepared, as my birthday was usually celebrated on that day, and they drank to my health. Jim made one of his funny, witty speeches, for he was as bright as a dollar and spoke English and French equally well. To all our surprise, Prov gave one gulp of his drink, his eyes filled with tears and, excusing himself, fled to his room.

Well, take in the situation if you can. Jim put down his head and gave a very low whistle. George looked daggers at me, saying, "Why in Heck did you let that guy come here?" Even poor, dear, sweet Mother, who never blamed me for anything, said, "Laura, you were very wrong in letting him come here under the circumstances." Well, we prevailed upon George to go and see if the man was sick and George took him over to his house across the yard.

It was a cold, blizzardly day and we couldn't get out of the house. Well, the afternoon dragged on in a constrained manner. Finally, I called Jim Theard aside and told him, "You have got to get that man to leave with you in the morning, or I'll never speak to you," and he promised he would do it. It was impossible to find out if he was leaving or not and I knew that all Charlie and I wanted was to get rid of Jim. Like the old bulldog he was when I asked him to do anything, Jim was determined to get Prov packing.

In the morning I got a note from Jim which said, "Hopeless." I told Mother to announce that I had a wretched cold and would probably have to stay in bed all day. Well, that did seem to do the trick as Prov then decided to leave.

As Prov and Jim were about to leave, I went to say goodbye. My conscience smote me. Prov had come such a distance to see me and then I should let him go without a word of comfort. So, I said, "As it is not raining, I will drive to the train with you."

Jim sat in front with the driver while Prov sat with me in back. As the train pulled in, Prov caught his satchel as if he had changed his mind to stay. Jim, too quick for him, grabbed the satchel, threw it on the platform and called, "Come on, old man, or you will miss that train." The last I saw of Prov, he was stamping on the back platform with his handkerchief to his face, while Jim had left him to go and relax with a cigarette.

I returned to the plantation home and did go to bed, worn out and exhausted, still being blamed by the family, most unjustly. Will McGary, true to his word, returned the next weekend to learn what he could never hear from me, for I was so like a clam about my affairs that my relatives had dubbed me *"Belle Mysterieuse."*

Will McGary did get the best of me in the cleverest way I ever could have imagined. He was positive he could win me by his constancy, and, as I knew that nothing could ever break his heart, it amused me. When I did tell him, some months later, of my engagement, he was dumb with surprise and, going on a business trip to St. Louis, called at Charlie's office to congratulate him.

Charlie was out so Will left a most complimentary note saying that he had known me a long while and wished to congratulate Charlie upon winning the "second loveliest woman in the world." It was the cleverest comeback I had known and enjoyed it immensely. The next time I saw him, neither of us said a word, but just looked at each other and shook with laughter.

Civil Marriage Registration for Charles Gore & Laura Locoul April 29, 1892

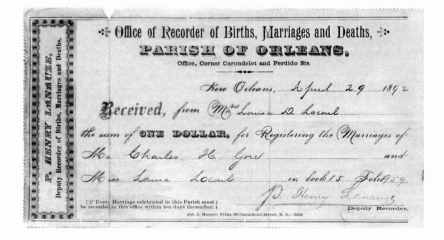

The announcement of my engagement fell like a thunder clap and astounded the entire community who little suspected the secret that lay buried six long years in my heart. God has now chosen to reward our patience and constancy. His Will be done and now happiness be our lot.

I had turned my back upon the past and the past seemed to me like a blank book. I could only look upon the future, to see the happiness that I trusted awaited me, coming to me, and I trusted to God's mercy to dispel the only cloud that would be caused by the separation from my loved ones and, especially, my own darling Mother.

The old plantation was sold on the 14th of March, 1891, for a mere song. We visited it for the last time to move out the contents and I left alone on the steamer "Whisper" with all my baggage on March 30th. I waved my last farewell from the boat and closed my eyes and cried.

BY HOEY & O'CONNOR.

The "Laura" Sugar Plantation,

IN THE PARISH OF ST. JAMES,

On the West Bank of the Mississippi River.

Also Accessible by the Texas and Pacific Railroad, Which Runs Through the Land, Adjacent to Which is Vacherie Station.

But 55 Miles from the City.

AT AUCTION.

ON LONG CREDIT AND LOW INTEREST.

BY HOEY & O'CONNOR—Nicholas J. Hoey, Auctioneer—Office No. 17 Carondelet street—SATURDAY, March 14, 1891, at 12 o'clock m., at the Auctioneers' Exchange, on St. Charles street, in this city of New Orleans, will be sold at public auction—

The "Laura" Sugar Plantation,

which contains 725 arpents, more or less, having a front of 6 arpents on the Mississippi River. There are about 110 acres of first year's stubble and about 125 acres of plant cane, a good sugar-house, complete in all its appointments, 26 mules and a full supply of carts, cultivators and other agricultural implements. TWO DWELLING HOUSES, stables, etc.

The land is famous for its productiveness and the situation is considered one of the most desirable in the sugar producing section.

Newspaper auction notice
for the sale of
Laura Plantation

"Duparc & Locoul Plantation"
watercolor by
Ivan de Lobel
1855

A
CREOLE FAMILY
ALBUM

A commentary
with photographs & illustrations
on the lives of the
Duparc, Locoul & de Lobel families of Louisiana
and the Charles Gore family of St. Louis, Missouri

GUILLAUME DuPARC
1752-1808
Revolutionary War Veteran

Philippe Guillaume Benjamin Gilles Duparc was, like many veterans, a man acquainted with conflict and violence. Born to a Norman family of distinction from Caen, a young and hot-tempered Guillaume brought disgrace on the Duparc family by killing a close friend of his father's in a duel. Guillaume's father, in seeking to regain his honor and punish his son, ran after him, shooting. He missed his target, but killed his favorite cow.

Manoir de Flagy,
the Duparc family home,
at Ste. Honorine du Fay,
south of Caen, Normandie

Although not physically injured, Guillaume was not to escape his father's wrath. He was banished from his family and sent to the *Marines Françaises*, at that time the watery equivalent of a fate worse than death. Initially assigned as an assistant gunner, this resilient and ambitious young Frenchman rose quickly in the ranks of the *Marines*. By crossing the Atlantic and fighting in the American Revolution, Guillaume would make a name for himself.

Before entering the *Marines*, Guillaume Gilles adopted the surname "desMessier Duparc," inferring some relation to nobility. Perhaps, in exile, he wanted to distance himself from his family or, rather, wanted to assign himself a cachet higher than that of his then lowly status. Whatever were his reasons, he soon became known by the name he chose: Duparc.

In the first campaign of his active military service, Duparc fought at the Battle of Savannah in 1778 under the French Admiral Charles-Henri d'Estaing. In 1780, his instincts found him under the Spanish General Galvez fighting the British at the Battle of Pensacola. At this naval engagement, Duparc and his trusted friend, Pierre Rousseau, were cited by King Carlos of Spain for their roles in this French/Spanish co-victory.

Guillaume Gilles Duparc

Duparc, never one to flee from adventure or mercenary reward, fought again for the French in 1781. Joining Admiral de Grasse in Haiti, Duparc sailed north to the Battle of the Outer Banks. Shortly after this expedition, his wartime career climaxed with de Grasse at the Battle of Yorktown, where Duparc was wounded.

When the Revolutionary War ended, Duparc and Rousseau were commissioned by the Spanish to defend His Catholic Majesty's Louisiana waterways. The two, in the employ of King Carlos, became partners in real estate and business ventures in Louisiana, buying property along the Mississippi River and in southwest Louisiana. Within a year, King Carlos awarded Rousseau for his service and named him *Commandante* of the post in Natchitoches.

It was through Rousseau that Duparc met his future wife. While Duparc was in Natchitoches on business, Rousseau, an in-law of the Creole Prud'Homme family, tactfully introduced Duparc to their very eligible daughter, Nanette. Duparc's marriage to Nanette in 1788 provided all the necessary financial, political and social base needed for his future well-being.

Admiral de Grasse

Duparc himself was later awarded the commandancy of the smaller Presidio of Pointe Coupée, a strategic outpost in central Louisiana. Military *commandantes* such as Rousseau and Duparc were paid with a pension, land and status in Spanish Louisiana. By 1792, Duparc had acquired all three.

The responsibilities of Spanish *commandantes* entailed governing both militarily and politically, a strange irony since Duparc had left France a few years before as a disgraced murderer. In similar fashion to other Spanish colonial officials, the Frenchman Duparc enforced Spanish law on a French and Creole populace, both free and slave, most all of whom, had preferred living under the French *drapeau*. Stationed at Pointe Coupée from 1792 until the Louisiana Purchase in 1803, Duparc is best remembered in history books as being responsible for the brutal suppression of the 1795 slave uprising that erupted on the plantations of Pointe Coupée.

With the Louisiana Purchase, Duparc was relieved of his command and, by 1804, Duparc had started a sugarcane plantation on the Mississippi River 50 miles above New Orleans. In his earlier real estate experience the war veteran had become familiar with this prime, high ground and bought out the poor Acadian farmers who owned it. And, in proper military fashion, Duparc had his plantation house surrounded by four iron cannons, each pointing to a cardinal point.

In 1808, before his first crop was sold, Guillaume Duparc, aged 52, died on the plantation, musket in hand, the owner of 27 pairs of white muslin pantaloons. In Duparc's Last Will, he gave the sugar *l'habitation* to his wife and children, at the same time admonishing the next generation by writing, "and, if my descendants intend to sell the plantation, I want them to sell it to a person who will be able to pay for it quickly, but above all, not to an American person, to avoid all trickery and bad chicanery to the members of my own family from this sort of people."

THE DuPARC HABITATION

Guillaume's sugar farming complex was originally called *l'habitation Duparc,* then, years later, Duparc Plantation and, after the Civil War, renamed the Laura Plantation. At its largest size it was approximately 12,000 acres, which included properties that had been amassed over time. In 1804, Thomas Jefferson was handing out Louisiana land grants. Jefferson heard about Duparc, a seasoned military man who hated the British and he accepted Duparc's petition for property. Jefferson's grant was beneficial to both parties. Duparc received a valuable plot of land and Jefferson secured Duparc's loyalty to the United States.

In addition to Jefferson's assistance, Duparc acquired adjacent parcels from Acadians who had settled the land twenty years prior. By the time of the Louisiana Purchase in 1803, arable land along the Mississippi River was limited and valuable. Many small, pioneer landowners jumped at the opportunity to sell their homesteads; others were forced to move by the wealthier, well-connected newcomers, such as Duparc.

Duparc's new farm was located on prime real estate, unusually high and cleared ground. He placed his plantation manor house squarely in the middle of the large Colapissa Indian village that had stood on-site for more than a century. In the Louisiana tradition, Duparc did not engage the Indians as laborers on his farm, but kept them on the plantation, perhaps for security reasons. The natives continued to live on the property, gradually migrating to the rear of the long (18 miles) tract, near the cypress swamps, where the last of their full-blooded descendants resided until 1915.

Construction of Duparc's manor house began in 1804 and was completed 11 months later. The work was executed by trained slaves, highly skilled in pre-fabricated methods that were typical of early Louisiana's vernacular structures. The slaves, probably of Senegalese descent, were rented for the construction, having been contracted from their New Orleans' masters.

In the typical Louisiana style, Duparc's manor house was raised high above ground resting on blue-grey glazed brick columns and walls, supported underground by an 8-foot deep pyramidal brick foundation. The cypress superstructure was inlaid with locally fired brick *(briqueté-entre-pôteaux)*, plastered inside, and stuccoed outside, with a brightly painted (red, green, ochre and pearl gray) exterior. This U-shaped structure totaled approx. 24,000 sq. ft. and had a 2,500 sq. ft. detached kitchen to its rear. By the time Duparc died in 1808, the *l'habitation* consisted of 10 sizable buildings, including quarters for seventeen slaves, a barn, warehouses and a small, rudimentary sugar mill.

Sugar Harvest in Louisiana
from Harper's Weekly
1875

Some 600 feet north of the manor house flowed the Mississippi River. A wooden pier allowed docking for boats of all sizes. Along the riverbank, ran a five to six foot-high *levée* that afforded protection from spring flooding. A primitive road followed the *levée* and a tall fence separated the plantation from passersby.

Inside this fence were planted two large orchards of pecan trees that parted to create an *allée*, where one could see the manor house from the river and, more importantly, funnel the river's breeze directly into the house.

The manor house, surrounded by a high fence, served not only as office headquarters for business but as the site for all manner of social entertainment. The *maison principale*, or "big house," as it was usually called, was later surrounded on three sides by added housing for the family members, overseers and contracted labor, as well as by barns and three carriage houses. The whole of the plantation was painted in a color code of ochre, red, green, mauve and gray, the same colors found on the manor house.

Approximately 400 feet behind the manor house was a road, going south, perpendicular to the river, lined on both sides with slave cabins facing the road and stretching a distance of 3.5 miles. This was always referred to as the "back" of the plantation, where the enslaved laborers resided, separated from the area around the manor house, called the "front," by a high fence and muddy swale that ran parallel to the river. Each cabin in the slave quarters held two family units and each had a chicken house and/or pig-pen and a vegetable garden just outside the cabin.

In the decades before the Civil War, the slave quarters consisted of sixty-nine cabins, communal kitchens, a slave hospital, and several water wells stationed along the road. One mile behind the manor house stood the sugar mill. It was surrounded, as everything else on the plantation, by sugarcane fields. By the 1850s, the Duparc Plantation was the workplace for 100 mules and 195 human beings, 175 of them slaves.

NANETTE PRUD'HOMME
1768-1862

nna "Nanette" Prud'Homme was born at Fort St. Jean-Baptiste in Natchitoches, a third generation Louisianian. Nanette's French-Canadian ancestors had emigrated from Québec with Iberville in 1699 to settle the Louisiana wilderness. Before coming to French Canada, Nanette's great-grandfather Prud'Homme had been court physician to the French King Louis XV. Such a noble connection ensured the Prud'Homme family a firm social standing in Louisiana under both French and Spanish rule.

Pierre Rousseau, Guillaume Duparc's comrade-in-arms, was the Spanish Commandante at Natchitoches when he introduced his cousin-by-marriage, Nanette, to the bachelor Duparc at a military ball. Guillaume was 32 and Nanette, delicate, but strong in character, was 20. Courtship ensued and they were married in Natchitoches in 1788. Nanette's Creole family was one of Louisiana's oldest and Duparc was a highly decorated and richly rewarded military hero. It was a marriage intended to be of social equals.

Nanette Prud'Homme Duparc

The couple's first years together were quiet, spent in the cotton farming region, not far from the Prud'Homme relatives' plantations and townhouses in Natchitoches. This is where their first child, Louis, was born. Nanette left Natchitoches when King Carlos IV of Spain appointed Duparc as *Commandante* of the Post of Pointe Coupée in central Louisiana. Here, where their next two children, Flagy and Elisabeth, were born, the life of a Spanish *Commandante* was one crisis after another; French and Spanish feuds, Indian and slave uprisings.

Abrupt change came with the Louisiana Purchase in 1803. Aided with land grants, the couple moved to their new plantation on the Mississippi River. Thirty months later, at age 41, Nanette was a widowed mother with 3 children and a sugar plantation with 17 slaves to operate.

Louisiana's legal code gave Nanette rights of inheritance as well as property rights. With these privileges, Nanette took control of the fledgling sugarcane enterprise, becoming the first of four generations of women to manage this plantation. In a period of 21 years, she had established the Duparc Plantation as a major producer of sugar, all the while diversifying the business into other crops, lumber and livestock, with great success. In 1829, at 61 years of age, Nanette retired, handing the plantation businesses to her three children.

Being a country girl at heart, and no longer a member of the plantation household, Nanette resisted the Creole imperative to leave the farm and live in New Orleans, a city she believed to be full of "clumsy, gauche and socially inferior Americans." So, she built her own retirement home, a 6,900 sq. ft. retreat house, just 500 ft. away from the plantation manor house, were she could live, albeit independently from the family business. Nanette called the place her *"maison de reprise,"* her house where she could start life all over again.

Detail of the
1808 succession
of Guillaume Duparc,
listing his
17 slaves

While residing "right next door," Nanette shrewdly negotiated with her children a unique settlement in which she would receive a payment of 1,000 *piastres* per year, which amounted to a sort of retirement or consultant stipend. In today's money, the amount equates to approximately $75,000 per year. Nanette resided for 33 years at her *maison*, living off her annual payment and attended by the same two female slaves, Henriette and Nina.

Maison de Reprise,
Laura Plantation
1919

In April of 1862, the Civil War came to the very gates of the sugar plantation. After capturing New Orleans, the Union Navy sailed upriver , shelling 40 plantation manor houses in St. James Parish, all whose owners had not signed the Oath of Allegiance to the United States. When the flotilla neared the Duparc property, the rest of the family fled, leaving the lame and senile Nanette with the slaves. The USS Essex bombarded the manor house, hitting the place four times. When the smoke had cleared, Nanette had disappeared, 94 years of age.

LOUIS de MEZIERE DuPARC
1789-1852

ashing, arrogant and belligerent, Louis was the first born of the Duparcs. At an early age, he gave evidence of his father's hot-natured temperament, so much so that even his friends began to call Louis the "Fire Eater." Nanette assumed that Louis would succeed her to manage the fortunes of the Duparc family. Nanette expected Louis to follow in Guillaume's footsteps, to enroll in the military and, one day, to manage the plantation. Louis was 18 when his father died. Nanette, who was left with the responsibility of running the sugar plantation, already had serious doubts about Louis' abilities.

Resolved to tame her son's aggression, Nanette shipped him off to the Royal Military Academy in Bordeaux hoping that he would return a polished gentleman. Away from his mother and flush with her hefty bankroll, Louis, though, preferred to party. It was in Bordeaux that he met his future wife, the vivacious German-born, Fanny Rücker. They married in France in 1812 and, two years later, Fanny bore Louis a beautiful daughter, Eliza.

With Eliza's birth, Louis' considerable Louisiana inheritance was secured. It was also time for him to repay the generous allowance his mother provided for him in France. Nanette withdrew all her financial support and summoned him home to the plantation. Nanette needed help in marketing the sugar business and feared that Louis would be swept up in the French war machine. With Napoleon in retreat from Moscow at the time, there was a real threat that Louis faced conscription into the French army.

Nanette realized her oldest son for the *bon-vivant* he was and, once back home in Louisiana, he was enlisted by Nanette to be her business agent in New Orleans. It was a perfect match, for Louis was ill-suited to the boring routine and isolation that was Creole plantation life. In New Orleans, Louis and Fanny held court at their new residence on Royal Street, the former "party house" of Felix Labatut. It was here where they conducted business and hosted gala balls. In short time, their reputation for lavish and extravagant behavior spread among Creoles and Americans alike.

Like his flamboyant father before him, Louis' fiery temper and ego were never satisfied. With his military training, Louis was always playing the week-end soldier and, by 1824, was named Brigadier General of the Louisiana Militia. He would relish this enviable role and his plum of a job in the family business until the great tragedy of his life occurred, seven years later, in 1831.

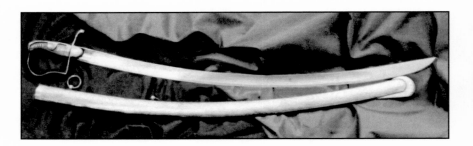

Louis Duparc's
sword & scabbard
ca. 1812

MARIE-ELIZABETH **FANNY RUCKER**
1789-1852

M. E. Duparc née Rücker

Charming and intelligent, Fanny Rücker brought a welcome change to the boisterous life of Louis Duparc. Born into a German middle class family in the shipping business, Fanny had been educated by governesses and in Paris finishing schools. She met Louis while visiting friends in Bordeaux, where he attended the military academy. After marrying in Paris in 1812, Fanny and Louis remained in France with a social life so busy that it was enough to strain Nanette's generous purse strings.

Upon their recall to Louisiana, the couple's partying did not cease and they were soon dubbed *"Marquis et Marquise de St. Jacques,"* a title derived from St. James Parish, the site the Duparc Plantation. Because "moderation was not one of the Creole virtues," the Duparc Plantation became known for its grand parties, as did the couple's residence on Royal Street and their home in Bordeaux.

Fanny brought a sophisticated elegance to the simple country home of the Duparcs. Friendships that the couple made in Bordeaux began a family network that expanded into a business partnership when Louis' sister, Elisabeth Duparc, married Raymond Locoul, also from Bordeaux. At the plantation, Nanette delegated the social protocol of the business to the young couple, having Fanny assume the role of hostess of the *l'habitation Duparc*.

Nanette realized that Fanny was a natural teacher and put to good use her daughter-in-law's European schooling. Upon arriving at the plantation, Fanny was made to pay special attention to the young Elisabeth, teaching her academic as well as social skills. And, when her own daughter, Eliza, was old enough, Fanny became her daughter's personal tutrix, repeating all the private lessons befitting an heiress. A generation later, Elisabeth's own daughter, Aimée, became the last of Fanny's pupils.

Silver teaspoon belonging to the Duparc family

127

ELIZA DuPARC
1814-1831

Eliza, Louis' darling daughter and the first grandchild in the Duparc family, was born to Fanny in Paris. She arrived with her parents at the plantation when she was two years old and was groomed as an heiress to the family fortune. Like her father before her, Eliza's lot was set, to take her place in society, to wed a suitable Creole or Frenchmen and inherit the plantation. These expectations created a great deal of pressure on her, burdens that all the pampering, spoiling and other outward signs of affection could not mask.

Doctor's bill
for Eliza Duparc's
medical
treatments

Eliza was pushed to be perfect, beautiful, intelligent and second-to-none. At age 16, she broke out with a skin condition, either acne or the shingles, and her parents could not allow it. Having no confidence in American doctors to cure the girl's skin problem, Fanny sought out the advice of her old friend and now brother-in-law, Raymond Locoul. Raymond referred Fanny to a skin specialist in Paris. The Duparcs sailed for the Continent, with Eliza and Raymond in tow. After a period of eight days of administering medication to Eliza, she fell dead.

Raymond Locoul was in an adjoining room when the tragedy happened and heard the doctor rush in and exclaim, *"Mon ami, j'ai fait une boulette!"* "My friend, I've made a miscalculation!"

Fully aware of Louis' violent nature, Raymond ran to Louis and Fanny to plead the doctor's innocence, convincing the shocked parents that the teenager's death was a result of cholera and that, if there were any blame, it was entirely theirs! The parents' guilt lay in their unmitigated vanity to make their daughter "perfect." Fortunately, Raymond's immediate intervention saved the doctor from Louis' vengeance.

Fanny had a death mask struck from which she had a portrait painted of her dead girl. Eliza would, forever, be perfect. The portrait showed a stunning, young woman with a flawless complexion. One year later, Louis and Fanny embarked for Louisiana with Eliza's body and interred her in a new family tomb ten miles upriver of the Duparc Plantation at the St. James Church cemetery.

Fanny took the death mask and the portrait, placed them on the mantel of her bedroom fireplace at the plantation and never set foot out of her room for the rest of her life! She told family and visitors that she had murdered Eliza for her own pride and that she needed to do penance for her sins. At 44 years of age, Fanny strictly cloistered herself, observing full mourning customs until her own death at the plantation twenty years later, in 1852, age 64. For consolation in her grief, Fanny had occupied herself for all those years with hours of prayer, sewing and with maintaining an active correspondence with her family and friends in France.

Duparc & Locoul tomb,
St. James Cemetery,
photograph taken
by Laura,
1931

In 1847, when Fanny was 57 years old, she wrote to a friend in Paris, saying, "I no longer expect anything pleasant in my life. That has been my destiny, always sorrows and anxiety. That is how I spend my life and I am utterly annihilated. I am sure that I will never be happy, ever again." Fanny found relief in tutoring her young niece, Aimée, but, for the most part, she would lose herself in literature, ordering hundreds of imported volumes by French authors, including the works of Alexandre Dumas and Honoré de Balzac.

For the tenure of Fanny's self-imposed incarceration, Louis left her, quitting the sugar plantation for his Royal Street residence where he lived for 18 more years, attended by two teenage slave girls. Louis Duparc died in the New Orleans cholera epidemic of 1850. Both Fanny and Louis were buried with Eliza, their only child.

FLAGY GILLES DuPARC
1792-1860

MERCELITE CORTEZ
1808-1850

Flagy, the younger son of Guillaume and Nanette, refused to be formally educated and rejected all efforts for him to make the "Grand Tour" of Europe. He was intensely jealous of his older brother, Louis, and feuded with him over every issue. All the while, Flagy relentlessly begged Nanette to be the overseer of the sugar plantation and, finally, she gave in to his pleadings.

For 30 years, Flagy faithfully managed the daily field operations of the Duparc business, first for his mother, Nanette, and then for his younger sister, Elisabeth. In 1829, during Flagy's stewardship, Elisabeth joined Flagy and their older brother, Louis, in forming a family partnership that would become one of Louisiana's leading sugar companies for almost 50 years.

At Nanette's urging, Flagy returned to Natchitoches to marry his family friend and 2nd cousin. Well-educated, unpretentious, and with a temperament as mellow as was Flagy's, Mercelite Cortez soon found herself on the plantation, managing domestic affairs of the Duparc manor. She was responsible for directing the house slaves, tending to their health and to their day-to-day problems.

Flagy and Mercelite resided on the plantation while other family members were away on business in New Orleans, enjoying the pleasures of society. The arrangement suited the quiet couple well since they were not as socially outgoing as the siblings. They rarely visited their Bourbon Street townhouse in New Orleans. Instead, they tended to the company books and cared for the aging Nanette. The tomb of Flagy and Mercelite stands today in the St. James Cemetery next to the tomb of Louis Duparc's family.

ELISABETH DuPARC
Her Early Years: 1796-1822

Elisabeth Duparc

The only daughter of an aristocratic colonial family, Elisabeth grew up in a privileged atmosphere. At the transfer of Louisiana to the U.S. in 1803, it was the seven-year-old Elisabeth who had the honor of lowering the French flag and of raising the U.S. flag at the ceremony in central Louisiana. Elisabeth was 12 years old when her father, Guillaume Duparc, died and she lived, for years afterwards, close to her mother, in the shadow of her father's death.

The Widow Nanette realized that Elisabeth had a keen intellect and was strong-willed. More and more, she relied upon Elisabeth to relieve her of the duties of running the sugar business. As a teenager, Elisabeth remained on the plantation, isolated from the other Creole *demoiselles* in New Orleans. Before her twentieth birthday, she was keeping records of business transactions and sharing with her mother the responsibilities of decision making.

Elisabeth's introduction into society was delayed by years of heavy, ritualized mourning and inhibited by the lack of a male family member to escort her through the social circles where she would, someday, meet a suitable marriage partner. Elisabeth's older brother, Louis, was in France, and Flagy had neither the graces nor inclination to look out for his sister's future.

When Elisabeth was 19, Louis finally returned from his long stay in France with his wife, Fanny Rücker. Fanny took to her younger sister-in-law with gusto and treated her as a young sister. In a short time, Fanny brought a gaiety back to the young, repressed Elisabeth and to the somber plantation household, as well.

Elisabeth was grilled in math and English by imported tutors. From her Aunt Fanny, Elisabeth learned about the latest fashions, the manners of European society and contemporary authors, artists and music.

By the age of 26, Elisabeth was still unmarried and very eligible. At a party arranged by Louis and Fanny, Elisabeth met Raymond Locoul from Bordeaux. The Frenchman had arrived with letters of introduction from family friends, a necessary formality for *entrée* into the tightly-knit Louisiana Creole community. After careful scrutiny by the Duparcs, this genteel and pleasant young man was accepted as a suitor. The couple married in 1822 at the Cathedral of St. Louis in New Orleans. Locoul had arrived from France just six months earlier.

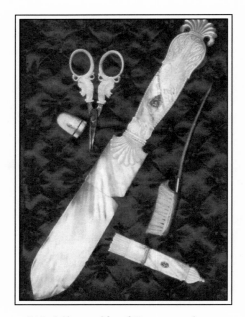

Wedding gift of Raymond to Elisabeth, 1822
Mother of Pearl toiletries and sewing items

GEORGE **RAYMOND LOCOUL**
1796-1850

[signature]

T he year 1821 saw the arrival in New Orleans of George Raymond Locoul, a polished gentleman and heir to the wine producing *Chateau Bon-Air* near Bordeaux, France. He came at the urging of his dear friend, Fanny Rücker, whose intention it was to match the Frenchman in marriage to her eligible and business-savvy sister-in-law, Elisabeth Duparc. Soon after Raymond arrived, Fanny arranged a meeting for him and Elisabeth to meet at the French Quarter home of the "prominent *Monsieur* Felix Labatut."

At their engagement, Elisabeth and Raymond signed a pre-nuptial agreement guaranteeing Elisabeth and her children from this union, all properties, rights and privileges which Raymond was bringing to the marriage. From Raymond's view, Elisabeth would be an excellent asset for managing his wine business. On her part, Elisabeth's dowry provided an amount of 7,000 *piastres* plus a promise to leave for France, as soon as possible, to run Raymond's business there. For Elisabeth, Raymond Locoul was a first-class ticket to escape the new America that she increasingly disdained.

Raymond Locoul
of Bordeaux

Locoul, though, as Laura writes, "was dropped in the midst of a family of fire eaters" and "managed to be the pacifist during the family arguments." It was this same man who, at the tragic death of Eliza, diverted Louis' anger, avoiding the doctor's murder.

In an effort to expand Locoul's wine market into Louisiana, Raymond and Elisabeth began in the 1830s to import Locoul's Bordeaux vintages. Under their direction, the Duparc Plantation became the largest wine distributor in Louisiana at the time, with a 10,000-bottle capacity.

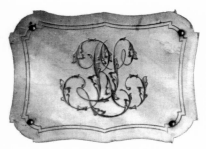

Raymond Locoul's initials "R.L."
on the brass plate of his 1821 traveling chest

Locoul Tomb,
St. Louis Cemetery,
New Orleans

Despite their early successes, Elisabeth's plans to move to France were put on indefinite hold as she found herself unable to leave the sugar plantation in the hands of her two incompetent brothers. With the establishment in 1829 of the *Duparc Frères et Locoul Sugar Company*, Raymond and Elisabeth renewed their attempts to make Louis and Flagy responsible partners in the family's business ventures. Their efforts were to no avail.

By default, Elisabeth eventually had to take over the reins of the sugar enterprise. For the next 20 years, Raymond conducted the family businesses from New Orleans and France, all the while, Elisabeth grudgingly managed the plantation with Flagy.

As the years passed, Louis and Elisabeth saw their chances to return to France fade. In 1847, Raymond wrote to a friend, "Oh, how I long for France. It is so sad to live so far away from my country. Maybe, one day we will be happy. Maybe, we will come back to the France we love so much and for which we felt so much pain to leave." Disheartened by their inability to quit Louisiana, Raymond and Elisabeth invested in New Orleans real estate, among their purchases, six residences in the French Quarter, one of them a house that was co-purchased with Louis Duparc.

In the 1850 cholera epidemic, which killed thousands in New Orleans, Raymond contracted the disease and quickly died. Because cholera was so contagious, Raymond's body could not be transported to the family tomb upriver in St. James. So, Louis Duparc had to bury Raymond in a new tomb in New Orleans and he then returned to the plantation with grim details of Raymond's death. Shortly thereafter, Mercelite Cortez, Flagy's wife, took ill, died at the plantation and was buried in the tomb in St. James that had been intended for Raymond Locoul. Louis, himself, died in the next epidemic of cholera and was buried next to his beloved Eliza in his tomb 10 miles upriver of the plantation.

THE CREOLE PLANTATION
IS A FAMILY BUSINESS

In the century before the untimely deaths of Raymond, Louis and Mercelite, Creole life in Louisiana exhibited a unique, characteristic thread: the understanding that the family was operated as a business and that the business was family. Whereas the family considered their French Quarter townhouses in New Orleans as their home, the plantation was where they went to work. The sugar plantation was central to their lives because it was the font from which every family member's income flowed.

Everyone in the family was a member of the business, each with his or her own accountable role. Early on, with Nanette in charge, *l'habitation Duparc* consisted of the immediate Duparc clan, with her three children and their spouses as officers. Apart from this nuclear family, the plantation workforce often included aunts, uncles, cousins and adopted or fostered children. As well, there lived on the place, men contracted as managers and overseers, with their families on-site, the plantation slaves and resident native Indians, all inhabitants of a nearly self-sufficient enterprise.

With each succeeding generation, Creoles, who already owned most of the valuable real estate in Louisiana, created businesses that encompassed a far-reaching network of cousins in related occupations and in politics. The Duparcs were a prime example of this, having family and commercial ties from Natchitoches in north Louisiana, on the Red River in central Louisiana, and along the Mississippi River plantation belt, down into New Orleans.

In a desperate attempt to break the stranglehold that Creoles held on Louisiana real estate, natural resources and the State's sugar/cotton-based economy, the Americans imposed, in the Code of 1824, a system of forced inheritance upon all citizens. The Anglo intent was to destroy the Creole estates, carving them into ever-smaller pieces and making them more available to American buyers. To thwart this American intrusion, the Creoles responded by forming family partnerships and corporation-like family enterprises. Clearly, this was the case when Elisabeth Duparc created, along with her two brothers, the *Duparc Frères et Locoul Sugar Company* in 1829.

While Creole Louisiana was defending itself from Anglo business interests, demand for Louisiana cotton and sugar created quick and vast fortunes for those plantations capable of meeting the sugar market's demand. In 1829, the Duparc family, searching for investment capital, divested itself of the Duparc estates in Normandy. With these funds the family renovated the plantation and were able to purchase state-of-the-art machinery for their sugar mill. By the 1840s, the plantation had seen 20 straight years of healthy profits.

Women making Sugar
Harper's Weekly
1853

When Nanette took over the family plantation in 1808, she started out with only 17 slaves. The number of slaves increased each decade. And, in 1830, when Elisabeth purchased additional sugarcane properties and commercial real estate in New Orleans, she also bought slave women for breeding stock for the plantation.

For leisure and business entertainment out on the plantation, the Duparcs extended their company railroad line beyond the sugarmill and through the cypress swamps, until it reached a party pavilion on the shores of Lake Des Allemands, seven miles distant.

THE ANTE-BELLUM YEARS
1823-1860

During these heady years of economic growth and Americanization, Elisabeth remained at the helm of the family and its business. Under her direction, the slave population of the plantation grew dramatically. She increased the cultivated acreage in sugarcane (at the same time included rice and cypress timber as cash crops) as well as other staples, enough to feed 200 people, as much as three meals a day. Elisabeth oversaw the flourishing wine distribution business and presided over all aspects of family life, both in the country and in New Orleans.

In the 1820s, with the unprecedented growth of the Louisiana sugar industry, the Duparc workforce had to expand. With hopes high, *Duparc Frères et Locoul Sugar Company* initiated in 1830 a slave breeding scheme, adding 30 females to their existing totals of 32 females and 60 males, to propagate and, ultimately, to provide the future labor force. In the sugar company's opinion, breeding slaves, like cattle, was much more economical than having to buy them. By the early 1840s, *Duparc Frères et Locoul* was awash in slave children. To house them, Elizabeth erected a new tract of 69 slave cabins, extending back, in double file, from 400 feet behind the manor house, back to a distance of over three miles.

By the 1830s, Nanette had retired and was living in her *maison de reprise*, where she grew steadily more senile. Éliza's untimely death sent Fanny Rücker into perpetual mourning and self-imposed confinement in the manor house. Then, with the sudden deaths of Raymond, Louis and Mercelite, a desperate Elisabeth was left alone to run the sugar plantation and the other family businesses. Elisabeth forced Fanny, though incarcerated in her bedroom, to supervise the running of the manor house. Flagy, grief-stricken for Mercelite, gave up his office in the manor house and tended the fields along with overseers appointed by Elisabeth.

Business necessitated that Elisabeth travel frequently between New Orleans and the plantation. For her long stays in the French Quarter, she was able to stay in the grand house on Toulouse Street behind the French Opera House that she and Raymond had purchased in 1835 from their sugarcane profits.

On Toulouse Street, surrounded by high brick walls, there was insulation from foreign influences. Elisabeth fought against any contamination of her children by the Anglos, a nearly impossible task since the children were exposed on a daily basis to the new, growing polyglot population of New Orleans. While the Old Guard Creoles retreated behind the iron grillwork of the French Quarter, the recent immigrants created a second city just a few blocks away where business was conducted in English, where gentlemen worked as lawyers and doctors, where democracy was considered valuable, public education was supported and where the Puritan ethic was overtly observed.

Signature of the
Widow Elisabeth Locoul

At the start of the Civil War, in 1860, *Duparc Frères & Locoul Sugar Company* owned 183 slaves living in 69 cabin dwellings. Of the property, 960 acres were planted in sugarcane and 1,134 acres were in cypress forest. The plantation had an assessed value of $80,000 with an additional $30,000 as the stated value of the machinery and implements. Of the farm animals listed, there were 10 horses, 75 mules, 15 milk cows, 25 oxen, 80 sheep, 30 swine and 30 cattle, with a total assessed value of livestock at $11,400.

The year's harvest of corn totalled 7,500 bushels and 100 bushels of sweet potatoes were harvested. Some 160 pounds of wool was sheared on the farm that same year. In addition, the sugarcane fields produced 460,000 pounds of granulated sugar and 30,000 gallons of molasses. Besides business items, the Duparcs and Locouls claimed $24,000 as the value of their personal belongings on the estate.

GEORGE RAYMOND **EMILE LOCOUL**
1822-1879

E mile Locoul was very much like his father, Raymond, and grew up a thoughtful, introspective child, not in the volatile Duparc tradition. Emile was strongly swayed in his early years by life in New Orleans, which, by then, was a bustling American city. With Anglos and immigrants arriving by the tens of thousands, New Orleans was in the throes of irreversible changes. For the first time since coming to the New World, the Duparc family and their culture were being invaded and overrun by the emerging American society.

While the majority of Emile's family resisted the new realities, he showed an open mind and was attracted to the vibrant, exciting ideas of the young United States. The remainder of the Duparc family, though, continued to find meaning and wealth in the Creole world. To remove him from these radical trends, Emile, just 13 years old, was sent to the Royal Military Academy in Bordeaux.

Raymond saw this as an opportunity for his son to become acquainted with the Locoul's Old World ties in Bordeaux and to relieve the stress growing between Elisabeth and their son. Elisabeth was disappointed that Emile was growing into what she deemed a weak, sensitive nature, what she referred to as a "negro spoiler." She hoped that Emile would, some day, become more like his militant *Oncle* Louis and his *Grandpère* Duparc and, in the process, be ready, when the time came, to assume the mantle of a disciplined plantation owner and Creole gentleman.

Once across the Atlantic, Emile found that France of the 1830s had changed drastically, as well. During the 20 years Emile spent there, he became immersed in the French *avant-garde*. He studied politics, art, literature, architecture and French sexual mores. He proudly counted among his friends the writer, Victor Hugo. Above all, Emile was intrigued by the French Enlightenment's ardent fascination with Law.

In backwater Creole French Louisiana, the legal profession was long considered an inappropriate pursuit for a young man of class. After all, law in Louisiana was American law and, although the French in France had become enamored with democracy, the Creoles were not. Lawyers in Louisiana were mostly Anglos and were considered by the Creoles to be hopelessly *bourgeois*.

In 1855, at 33 years of age, Emile completed his Grand European tour and returned eagerly to Louisiana. His heart was set on becoming a lawyer but his still grieving, widowed mother would have nothing of it. Elisabeth made it clear to Emile that, if he embarrassed the family by practicing law in Louisiana, she and his sister, Aimée, would force the sale of the family businesses, move to France and leave him to ply court cases in greatly reduced circumstances.

Confused and depressed by his mother's ultimatum, Emile put his lawyer's mind to work and realized that there was a way out of his dilemma. In Creole Louisiana, marriage and an heir would give him the lawful recourse that he needed against Elisabeth's threat of disinheritance.

Ironically, it would be Elisabeth who would provide Emile with the opportunity he was looking for. Arriving late to one of Elisabeth's dinner parties, Emile met Désirée Archinard, twice his cousin, seated at his mother's table. After months of courtship, they were married at Désirée's mother's house, "Oakland," on the Prud'Homme plantation outside Natchitoches.

To their Prud'Homme relatives at Oakland Plantation, Elisabeth and her daughter, Aimée, fawned excitement about the marital plans. But, on the plantation, Emile's marriage to Désirée was met with bitter dismay as the family had "all hoped he would remain a bachelor." His mother and sister now knew they had only one excuse to deny Emile. He would have to produce a child in order to salvage his future and inherit his $6.5 million share of the family fortunes.

Photo brooch of
Emile Locoul,
an engagement gift
to his fiancée, Désirée

MARIE ELISABETH **AIMEE LOCOUL de LOBEL**
1826-1880
In Her Mother's Footsteps

Aimée, like her older brother, Emile, was also born on the family plantation. She grew up a lonely, homely child in a house darkened by the tragedy of Eliza, the only other young girl in the family. Soon, Aimée was the over-protected pet of her Aunt Fanny, Eliza's mother.

Tante Aimée Locoul de Lobel

With Fanny in perpetual mourning, Elisabeth had Aimée visit Fanny in her cloistered bedroom to be tutored. Despite such a schoolroom, Aimée developed from Fanny a cultivated taste for the arts, for music, literature and things French.

Accompanying her mother on a business trip to France in 1855, Aimée met a French gentleman of culture, intelligence and social standing, attributes that characterized her late father, Raymond. With Elisabeth's approval, Aimée, at age 30, married Charles Ivan Flavien de Lobel de Mahy, an aristocrat of dwindling means. The newlyweds came to Louisiana on a honeymoon visit and then returned to live at the de Lobel houses in Lille and Paris, where Aimée bore three children. All the while, it was Aimée's substantial dowry that maintained the de Lobel's lifestyle and status.

Signature of
Charles Ivan Flavien de
Lobel de Mahy

Because of *Monsieur* de Lobel's recognized skills in engineering, Elisabeth urged the couple to come to America to put his award-winning expertise to good use in modernizing the Duparc sugar mill machinery. When they arrived in Louisiana, de Lobel's initial hopes and design plans had to be put on hold. Louisiana's entire economy was then paralyzed by the imminent threats of secession and civil war.

The de Lobels, sensing the impact this would have on all the planters' futures, urged Elisabeth to sell the sugar plantation. Concerned with their personal safety and with salvaging whatever they could of the family fortune, Aimée pressed hard upon Elisabeth to return to Paris where, together, they could live out their days in the leisure for which Elisabeth had toiled for so many years. Elisabeth found much of value in Aimée's offer and gave her approval to the de Lobel scheme.

DESIREE ARCHINARD LOCOUL
Changing the Balance of Power

Désirée Locoul

ésirée was born in Natchitoches, the cradle of Louisiana's rural Creole life, into the very family from which Nanette Prud'Homme came. She grew up a fourth generation Creole, surrounded by the classic conventions of a proper Creole lady. Like her mother before her, Désirée was schooled by the *Mesdames* of the Sacred Heart in Natchitoches. From the nuns she learned Catholic virtues and morals. From the many cousins and friends with whom she was in constant association on the cotton plantations around Natchitoches, she learned social graces, music, dance and endless burdens of hospitality amid the pleasures of countless parties, picnics and banquets. Somewhere, at an early age, she developed a life-long sophistication for fine fashion.

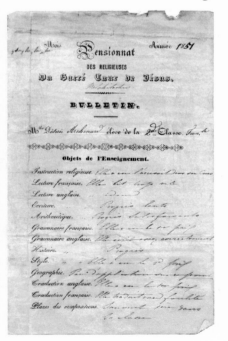

Désirée Archinard's report card 1851

From her family, she learned self-discipline in adversity, self-composure and dignity in grief, responsibility and adaptability to need, the primacy of family, the devotion to children and allegiance to tradition. Such ideals were imbedded into Désirée by the successful and extraordinary sacrifices made by the women in her family, by her sister and grandmother and, most notably, by her own beloved mother, Céphalide Metoyer.

In the isolation of the cotton fields around Natchitoches, the Creoles were content to live among themselves in year-long schedules of family dinners, outings, religious devotions and inter-marriage. By the Civil War, the waves of American encroachment had made little impact on the *Côte Joyeuse*. And, even though Désirée often visited New Orleans and her cousins on the Duparc plantation, she was, at age 19, still the unspoiled, country cousin of Emile when she first caught his attention.

To the marriage contract, Désirée Archinard brought a promissory note for $2,000. For his part, Emile brought $10,000 and a 17-year old mulatto house slave, named Louise, for his bride. Following her wedding, Désirée was awakened to the full extent of the Locoul family feud and the ultimatum placed upon her husband by Elisabeth. Désirée found Emile isolated from his own family and she his only support. On their honeymoon trip to France, Emile promised to show her the world. Instead, Désirée was shocked by her new de Lobel in-laws and their life style which she saw as hypocritical, affected and frivolous.

Désirée would also surprise Emile. Moving beyond her protected innocence and demure façade, she quickly displayed a strong-willed nature, advising Emile on how to handle his mother and sister and in prodding him to again pursue his lifelong dream in the legal world.

After settling in at the Duparc-Locoul plantation, she emerged as the decision-maker of the two, all the while playing the quiet role of devoted, practical wife and in-law. Together, the two newlyweds formed a partnership, one that was able to match that of Elisabeth and the in-law de Lobels. Wasting no time, Désirée had three quick miscarriages. Her fourth pregnancy gave Emile an heir who, just by her birth, determined the outcome of the family struggle.

Désirée Locoul and 3 month-old Laura

CIVIL WARS 1861
Two Houses Divided

By the time the first bombs fell at Fort Sumter, Désirée Locoul had conceived for the fourth time. Because of three earlier miscarriages, Désirée was confined for the full term of her pregnancy to the Duparc plantation. There, her first child, Laura, was born on a cold, calm Christmas Eve night, an event which would forever decide the family's future. The War Between the States, which had been brewing for over a decade, was now engaged. Likewise, with the birth of Laura, the chronic struggle between the Locouls and the de Lobels, who lived, worked and ate together on the plantation daily, reached the boiling point.

On one side of the fray stood Elisabeth, the legal owner of a farm she wanted desperately to sell but, because of pre-war hysteria, could not. Emile's sister, Aimée, allied herself with Elisabeth and together they refused to relinquish control to Emile because Elisabeth considered him an inadequate and weak manager. And, now that he had an heir, Elisabeth could not escape the inevitable division of her business property.

Emile stood on the other side in this family feud and, in the Creole understanding, had full right to his share of the family estates. Emile, though, was incapable of defying his controlling mother, even when it meant denying himself his dream of becoming a lawyer. But his marriage to Désirée and the birth of his little girl, Laura, dealt Elisabeth a definitive blow, drowning her own life-long hopes of leaving the plantation and retiring in France.

Elisabeth and Emile were stalemated when, in April of 1862, the Federal Gunboat Essex sailed upriver and bombed the manor house. Elisabeth escaped to Pointe Coupée; the de Lobels had already fled to France. Emile secreted Désirée and Laura off to the Prud'Homme plantation near Natchitoches, only to return to the River Road to head up the rebel St. James Guards militia.

For the remainder of the War, only the slaves and, later on, the Union soldiers remained on the plantation. With the surrender of the Southern armies in April 1865, Emile, who was seen by many locals as a war hero, went up to Natchitoches to retrieve Désirée and Laura and return to the Duparc-Locoul plantation to resume the inheritance struggle with his mother and sister.

THE PLANTATION IS RECONSTRUCTED
Post War Years: 1866-1874

During the Civil War, all the slaves of the *Duparc Frères et Locoul Sugar Company* remained on the place and showed no intentions of leaving. And, when the hostilities had concluded, all these formerly enslaved men, women and children were present to see the return of the Locouls and de Lobels. Elisabeth, who had previously taken the Oath of Allegiance to the United States, and the de Lobels, Aimée, Ivan and three children, found their way back to the plantation in 1865 and attempted to re-start the year-long schedule of sugar production. But, a year later, in 1866, when Emile and his family returned, they were shunned and regarded as interlopers by Elisabeth and the de Lobels. What, at first, looked to be a continuation of the pre-war family stand-off, though, was not to be.

Bonfire on the Levée
1871
From far right to left:
Eugénie de Lobel
with hair down to her knees,
Aimée de Lobel
Désirée Locoul
Noemie Locoul,
servant girl,
Ivan de Lobel

Unknown to Elisabeth and Aimée, Emile had been conducting maneuvers of his own. Realizing that war was imminent, Emile had hidden $2,000 in gold with a banker friend in New Orleans. En route to the plantation after the War, Emile recovered his cache and made the Duparc Plantation, at that time, one of the very few producers of sugar in America. From 1866 through 1868, the cost of sugar had skyrocketed and the Duparcs netted $75,000 each year, an enormous sum at the time. For the first time in his life, Emile realized that he had leverage over his mother. And, in her generosity, Elisabeth gave her two children gifts of $10,000 each from the profits.

After these successful years, Aimée again begged Elisabeth to sell the plantation and to use the profits to retire in France. Unwilling to entrust the plantation to anyone else, and unable to sell it without Emile's consent, Elisabeth, in 1872, reluctantly divided the farm between her two children. Emile, the elder child, was given first choice. He chose the half with the manor house, 3,000 acres and a promise from Elisabeth to give him the money needed to build his own sugar mill. Aimée received the other half with the sugar mill, and Elisabeth semi-retired to her French Quarter Toulouse Street mansion. Emile would never see the money that Elisabeth promised him to build his mill.

In Emile's first year, 1873, he produced a bumper crop. When he approached Aimée, asking her to process his cane at her mill, she and her husband, in collaboration with Elisabeth, stalled. Emile was forced to wait until December, when a hard freeze destroyed the bulk of his cane. Now, at last, Elisabeth and the de Lobels saw hope that Emile's loss would force him to sell. Désirée, who could see that no help from Elisabeth was forthcoming, pushed Emile into begging his old New Orleans friends for financial support. With a mortgage on his plantation in hand, Emile built a new sugar mill in 1874. To celebrate its opening, Emile threw a grand party at the manor house, inviting his entire family and the young girl friends of his 13-year old daughter, Laura.

Each *demoiselle* was instructed to bring to the party a suggestion for a name for the newly-built mill. Laura's best friend and cousin, Lily LeGendre, offered the name: "the Laura Mill." Realizing the opportunity at hand, Emile, in front of Elisabeth and Aimée, declared that his half of the old Duparc Plantation would henceforth to changed to the name: "The Laura" Plantation.

The naming of the new sugarcane farm marked the end of the long-held family feud. Whatever hard feelings persisted would be tempered by the times and circumstances to come. In the year that followed, Elisabeth fully retired to her Toulouse Street townhouse and Aimée and her family moved off the Duparc Plantation side into a small manor house some 2 miles downriver.

Désirée blossomed as mistress of the Laura Plantation, helping Emile as his behind-the-scenes business manager. With his wife playing a major role at the plantation, Emile was finally able to dedicate himself to his life-long passion: the law. Having been denied the freedom to pursue a legal career, Emile found the time to begin participating in local politics. With his leadership during the War years well known, Emile ran for State Representative for St. James Parish and was elected and re-elected, for a total of eight years. During these years his health was deteriorating, abetted by his constant smoking, drinking and narcotics prescriptions.

As the Louisiana sugar industry declined, Emile was forced to mortgage the plantation and he compounded his dwindling finances by racking up large gambling debts. By the time Désirée was able to get him good medical care, it was too late. Emile Locoul died, aged 56 years.

"THE LITTLEST REBEL"
LAURA LOCOUL

On Christmas Eve, 1861, nine months after the Civil War ignited, Laura Locoul was born into a family and a nation at war with itself. She was, at an early age, aware that her birth precipitated her own family being at odds with itself. By age 13, Laura felt a another heavy burden fall her slender shoulders when she was told by her father, Emile, that he wanted her to be the next president of the family's sugarcane plantation.

Laura grew up in the Creole tradition where duty-bound women found fulfillment in sacrificing themselves for the sake of their families, not in following their personal dreams. At the earliest age, Laura was immersed in what was expected of her. First, there was Désirée, her mother, who selflessly devoted her married life to solving Emile's family and business problems. Secondly, Elisabeth was Laura's sole role model as a plantation president. In her grandmother, Laura could see a woman who had become hardened by the lifelong responsibility of keeping family and business together. And, then, Laura was well versed in Désirée's saintly mother, Céphalide, her Aunt Irène and grandmother Aurore Lambre, whose lives were held up as the epitome of womanhood and Christian virtue.

As Laura saw it, her choice was simple. She could either acquiesce to Creole tradition, just as her forebears had done, or she could find her own individual self-fulfillment as an American. In 1875, at age 14, Laura asked Emile to send her away to school in New Orleans, so that she could learn the more liberal American customs of modern, young women. Reluctantly, Emile gave his permission and Laura lived in New Orleans, as far away as possible from the plantation, for 10 months of every year, for the next 4 years, until the day her father died.

*Désirée,
George
&
Laura Locoul,
1865*

Laura was 18 years old when Emile passed away. Under Désirée's guidance, Laura managed the sugar plantation for several years, bringing in overseers to run the day-to-day operations. For the first years, harvests were lean, the head overseer was ineffective, and the price of raw sugar remained perilously low. Laura and Désirée decided to appoint George, Laura's brother, at age 20, to administer the farm.

Laura Locoul
in silk ball gown
1890

Quickly, it became evident that George was not up to this task and, so, Laura took back the reins of the company. For the next four years, she tried to make a go of the farm, selling off large portions of the property to pay old gambling debts that Emile had accumulated. All the while, her heart was elsewhere.

With the Locoul's listed in the National Social Register, Laura never missed an opportunity to take part in high society. In New Orleans, she reveled in social galas and carnival balls. For months at a time, she traveled to New York and to posh resorts, hobnobbing with the wealthiest of Americans.

On one such vacation excursion in 1885 she met a gentle heir to a St. Louis family fortune, Charles Gore, and became secretly betrothed to him. Two months after Laura announced her engagement in 1891, both halves of the old plantation were auctioned; Laura's side selling for the meager sum of $20,500.

By the time of the act of sale, both Aunt Aimée and Ivan de Lobel had died and their three children had become French citizens. Eugénie moved to France, Fanny married the French Consul in New Orleans and Raymond became the French Consul in Seattle. In the sale of her farm, Laura stipulated that the farm, thereafter, always be called "Laura." In June, 1892, aged 29 years old, she married Charles Gore and moved to St. Louis, Missouri where she lived for 72 years, still near the banks of the Mississippi.

THE GORE FAMILY
OF ST. LOUIS

In marrying Charles H. Gore, Laura Locoul gave up the excesses of Catholic Creoles to live within a white-Anglo-Saxon Protestant family. The Gores were, for generations, mainstream Americans. Charles was from a family of prosperous St. Louis businessmen and entrepreneurs who called fashionable "Dillon Place" home. Prominence followed them as they were relatives of the family of Gov. Christopher Gore of Massachusetts and of Stephen Decatur, naval hero of the War of 1812.

On Charles' maternal side, the Helfenstein family was similarly entrenched in St. Louis society and Missouri business circles. When the German Helfenstein family immigrated to Missouri, they were already monied and educated and, once in St. Louis, became prosperous in the wholesale food and mercantile businesses. Above all, they would be known as strict Presbyterians.

At the start of the Civil War, the Gore family, with Charles and his older brother, Stephen Decatur Gore, left St. Louis and moved to England for their safety. After 6 years there, the family returned to their home on Dillon Place. Charles was considered by his family to be a sickly child and Anna Helfenstein, his mother, had Charles enrolled for 10 years in classes under Dr. Jacob Mahler, Sr., a noted dance master in St. Louis. Throughout these years, he was subjected to Dr. Mahler's short whip because he was not as good a dancer as was Stephen Decatur, his brother.

Charles &
Stephen Decatur Gore
1858

153

Charles finished his formal education at Washington University in St. Louis and immediately began work at the family-owned business, the Missouri Glass Company. As he was not physically cut out for such "confining" labor, he asked his father for part of his inheritance so that he could strike out for the West and make there his own fortune, as so many young men his age were doing.

Old Mr. Gore agreed and Charles, together with his good friend, Asby Chouteau, bought a cattle ranch near Deadwood, South Dakota. In the first winter, their entire cattle herd was lost to the cold and he returned home to St. Louis, dejected and broke.

Charles Gore
in
South Dakota
1884

It was just after this calamity that he was introduced to Laura Locoul at the wedding of their mutual friends, Jeannie Lockwood and Walker Hill. In quick succession, Charles was able to secure employment in the St. Louis branch of the Preferred Accident Insurance Co. of New York and then, propose to Laura. Partly because of his financial problems, Charles and Laura decided to keep their engagement secret for 6 years. During this time, Charles was promoted several times until in 1890 he was named the Missouri manager of the insurance firm.

THE ST. LOUIS YEARS
1892-1963

The wedding of Laura Locoul to Charles Gore took place on April 27th, 1892 at the bride's townhouse on Bourbon Street. It was an elaborate affair with both Catholic and Presbyterian ministers in attendance. At Laura's right-hand side stood the Locoul's former slave and Laura's nurse since birth, Anna. The newlyweds returned from their honeymoon in Atlantic City to live with Charles' brother and his widowed father and grandfather, all the while catered to in the big family home by "two splendid German women who kept house."

This arrangement became uncomfortable for Laura so she and Charles moved away to their first home on Finney Avenue. Here in 1893, Laura gave birth to Laura Anna Gore, from then on known as "Lollie."

That same year, Laura was visited by her cousin, Powhatan Clark, his wife and three-month old son. While swimming with Laura and Lollie, Powhatan dove into the water, struck his head against a rock and was killed. Overcome with grief, Mrs. Clark begged Laura to take her infant until she recovered. For the next five years, "little Powie III" was treated as another sibling in the Gore household in St. Louis.

*Laura, Désirée
and Lollie
1893*

The Locoul family
in 1894
George, Laura, Mimi
Lollie and Désirée

Three years later, Laura and Charles built a new residence at 4252 McPherson Ave. where Désirée, known as "Daisie" and Charles, Jr., called "Charlie" were born. Here, Stephen Decatur Gore, the inveterate bachelor, came to live with his brother's family.

Laura with
Daisie & Lollie
1897

156

Separation from her New Orleans family and friends was felt more deeply by Laura than she had imagined. Letters to her mother were frequent and always expressed the pain of her homesickness. Désirée, in turn remained equally troubled at the absence of her daughter and of Laura living without the constant and accustomed companionship of suitable women. So, Désirée visited Laura in St. Louis every year and, Laura, with her growing family in tow, made return treks to Louisiana.

*Désirée and
Lollie
1898*

Ever since the wedding in 1892, George, Laura's brother, had lived with Désirée and Mimi at their Bourbon Street house. Throughout his twenties, George was able to secure temporary employment, but never held a job that brought in enough to pay the living expenses for the three of them. Often, he was hired as a clerk or runner or office boy, only to change jobs within a year or so. He never married and displayed little or no interest in the opposite sex. Likewise, Mimi never held a job nor ventured far from her mother. She was not known to entertain suitors nor have her own coterie of friends. Living arrangements at 35 Bourbon Street remained relatively unchanged for the 13 years after Laura left.

By 1900, the French Quarter had become run down, with sorely depressed property values and the area was no longer a desirable neighborhood in which to live. In 1905, Laura pleaded with Désirée to leave New Orleans and to come and live near her in St. Louis. The offer was accepted, the townhouse sold and the last of the Locouls, Désirée, Mimi and George, left Louisiana for their new home on Maryland Avenue in St. Louis.

Laura & Charlie Jr.

*Laura and Daisy
on vacation*

Once settled in, the old pangs of separation eased for everyone. Stephen Decatur found George a position, menial though it was, at the Missouri Glass Company. Désirée happily became a doting grandmother and welcomed her baby-sitting duties for Lollie, Daisie and Charlie, Jr. She was especially pleased to be able to assist her grand-daughters in their Catholic schooling. Several years previously, Laura, in truest Creole fashion, had enlisted Lollie and Daisie in the Sacred Heart Academy in St. Louis. These two girls would be taught by the same order of Catholic nuns as Désirée and Laura's dear grandmother, Céphalide Metoyer, had been taught in Natchitoches.

Even though, by marriage, Laura had joined into a Presbyterian family, she had promised, as was the practice of Catholics in mixed marriages, to remain in her Faith and to raise her children in the Roman Catholic Church. Laura kept to her vow and lived out her life as a devout Catholic, all the while shielding her two daughters from the flirtations of young Protestant Anglos. George, Mimi and, of course, Désirée remained staunch Catholics, for as long as they lived.

In St. Louis, the Locouls and the Gores remained a tightly knit family and, every year, Laura and Charles invited Désirée, George and Mimi to join with them and the children in family outings and during vacation trips, Désirée especially enjoying their summer stays at her favorite getaway: Old Sweet Springs.

On the beach
1907
Lollie, Daisie,
Charlie Jr. and
Grandmother
Désirée

Désirée Archinard Locoul
1910

In 1911, Laura's beloved mother, Désirée, died and was buried in Calvary, the Catholic cemetery, in St. Louis. Laura's grief was soon to be compounded by Mimi's increasingly erratic behavior. Always introverted as a young girl, the sensitive Mimi fell into a long depression following her mother's death. Her mental health was questioned and she suffered frequent and more severe bouts of hysteria. In 1912, Mimi was married, aged 44, to her cousin, Neuville Prud'Homme.

Mimi was given her third of the Locoul inheritance including her share of the family furniture and she left St. Louis with Neuville to live at the family's Magnolia Plantation near Natchitoches, where he was the overseer. With Mimi gone, George found himself alone in Désirée's house. He had never married and, for the first time in his life, George moved out to live in his own apartment on Westminster St. and continued his job as office clerk and porter for the family's glass company.

After Désirée's death, Charles Gore's health became a factor about which Laura worried a great deal. On his doctor's advice, Charles semi-retired and began to spend weeks or, sometimes, months at a time away from St. Louis. He was warned that his health was jeopardized by the hot weather and he spent his summers much further north. This prescribed regimen was hard on his family, but, for Charles, it was an opportunity to follow his life-long passion for fly-fishing. From then on, there was many a summer that Laura and the children could be found standing along the chilly waters of Minnesota and Canada.

Charles Gore
and his
catch of the day,
1914

With so much time spent away from work, Charles realized that his position in the Preferred Insurance Company would, less and less, be able to pay for the lifestyle to which he and Laura were previously accustomed. So, when the note on the McPherson Avenue home had been paid, Charles, and with reluctance on Laura's part, invested what was left of his inheritance and much of Laura's, as well, into stock in the Pierce Gold Mining Co. of Denver, Colorado. Within twelve months, the value of his shares had collapsed.

Veiled Prophet Ball
1915

Stephen Decatur Gore stepped in to ease the shock. In 1915 and 1916, Uncle Stephen saw to it that Lollie and Daisie made their debuts at the Ball of the Veiled Prophet, of which Stephen was a charter member. The Veiled Prophet organization remains, to this day, a St. Louis societal landmark, similar to the old-line Carnival krewes (clubs) to which Laura's family belonged in New Orleans.

Uncle Stephen continued to live in the same house with Laura and Charles. Although he had become completely deaf, Stephen was always generous to the Gore children and shared his part of the Gore wealth whenever the need arose. Lollie and Daisie stayed at home, faithfully tending to both of their ailing parents. In 1918, Laura's own Charlie, Jr., aged 18, enlisted to fight in the war effort.

In 1922, Charles Gore died, a victim of arteriosclerosis. Laura was a widow at age 61. She had been in poor health before Charles' death and now, she relied even more upon Lollie and Daisie to care for her. In 1928 Stephen Decatur died. In his Will, he left part of his inheritance to Laura's children.

As the family fortunes dwindled, Laura began to sell off Locoul family heirlooms, furniture, silver and jewels. In 1928, she sold the family house on McPherson and moved into a smaller apartment nearby on deGiverville Street. There, in a much humbler place, she lived with Lollie and Daisie, surrounded by what had not been sold of the furniture, family photographs and plantation memorabilia.

In the summer of 1931, Laura, accompanied by her three children and by Charlie, Jr.'s wife, Hildegarde, rode in Charlie's car down to New Orleans. There, Laura pointed out to them the places that she had known so well. Finally, they traveled upriver to the old sugar plantation. For the first time, her children saw the "Laura Plantation." Throughout their trip, Laura recounted innumerable stories about her life and that of the children's ancestors.

The Gore family in 1918
Charlie Jr., Daisie, Stephen,
Charles, Lollie & Laura

163

Upon returning to the house on deGiverville Street, she began, at age 70, to write down what memories, recently jostled, remained of those earlier days. In the next year, George, then aged 68, came to live with Laura, Lollie and Daisy. For the next five years, Laura worked on her memoirs, aided by George's own recollections. In 1936, she completed her <u>Memories</u>, subsequently adding notes, pasting paragraphs and squeezing remarks into the margins, as she recalled them at the moment.

Laura Locoul Gore
1936

Sad news arrived from Natchitoches. Mimi had to be forcibly taken in the middle of the night from the Magnolia Plantation and institutionalized. She was placed in the insane asylum at Jackson, Louisiana and remained there until her death in 1944.

Lollie and Daisie never did marry but, in 1934, Charlie, Jr. wed Hildegarde Stoeckley. They had one son, Stephen Decatur Gore, Jr., who is Laura's sole living descendant.

In 1950, George Locoul, aged 86, was becoming a burden to Laura and he was sent to the Home for the Aged in St. Louis, operated by the Little Sisters of the Poor. He died there three years later. He was buried next to his mother, Désirée, at Calvary cemetery.

By the time of George's death, Laura was 91 years old and a frail woman who had difficulty in walking. Lollie and Daisie Gore remained with their mother, taking daily care of her and receiving counsel from Laura on what they should do for themselves after Laura's death with the remainder of the family monies and belongings. Neither of the two daughters were ever employed in any full-time job. As the years passed, they were unable to continue giving their volunteer time for charitable causes, as they had done in the decades before. For the rest of Laura's life, Lollie and Daisie were, for all intents and purposes, house-bound with Laura as her nursemaids.

Each year on Laura's birthday, December 24th, the children would give a festive party for friends and family in her honor. On her 100th birthday in 1961, Cardinal Ritter, of St. Louis, paid Laura a visit at her home. Laura, still quick-witted, jokingly admonished His Eminence in her conversation when she said, "You know, meeting you is nothing new to me, because down in Louisiana at our old plantation, we had the bishops there all the time."

In St. Louis on June 8th, 1963, Laura Locoul Gore died, 101 years old. She was buried, next to her husband, at the Gore gravesite in Bellefontaine, the Protestant cemetery in St. Louis.

John Cardinal Ritter
greeted Laura
on her 100th birthday
December 24, 1961

Behind the last leaf of Laura's "Memories" was found an inserted page, written shakily in her handwriting, unsigned and undated. It certainly must have been scribbled in the last years of her life. The note reads:

Looking back upon the past, I have had many ups and downs.
The downs seemed very hard to bear when they came.
And, when the ups appeared,
I usually forgot the cares and sorrows of the past.
Summing up my life,
I feel I have much to be thankful for.
I was blessed with friendships that were priceless to me.
I was surrounded by love always;
The worship of my father and mother,
the truest and most perfect love of my husband
and the sweetest consideration and love of my children.
God bless them all.
And, to dear, old Louisiana, the land of my birth,
I love you and am true to you still.